# Redefining Excellence

# Redefining Excellence

## THE FINANCIAL PERFORMANCE OF AMERICA'S "BEST-RUN" COMPANIES

Arabinda Ghosh

PRAEGER

New York
Westport, Connecticut
London

**Library of Congress Cataloging-in-Publication Data**

Ghosh, Arabinda
  Redefining excellence : the financial performance of America's
  "best-run" companies / Arabinda Ghosh.
      p.  cm.
    Bibliography: p.
    ISBN 0-275-93339-3 (alk. paper)
    1. Corporations—United States—Finance—Case studies.  2. Peters,
  Thomas J.  In search of excellence.  I. Title.
  HG4061.G46  1989
  658.1'5'0973—dc19          89-3859

Library of Congress Catalog Card Number: 89-3859
ISBN: 0-275-93339-3

First published in 1989

Praeger Publishers, One Madison Avenue, New York, NY 10010
A division of Greenwood Press, Inc.

Printed in the United States of America

The paper used in this book complies with the Permanent
Paper Standard issued by the National Information Standards
Organization (Z39.48—1984).

10 9 8 7 6 5 4 3 2 1

To the memory of my mother

# Contents

# Tables

# Preface

Although Thomas Peters and Robert Waterman's book *In Search of Excellence* was published in October 1982, it has been a perennial best seller ever since, and has become what *People* magazine has called "A Business Bible." But no matter whether these firms are "excellent" or not, they are mostly major U.S. companies such as General Motors, Exxon, IBM, Du Pont, etc., and together with the comparative "control" group of firms studied in the present work, constitute over 30 percent of the business activities in a given year. Thus to analyze the financial performance of these firms during the last twenty-five years (1960–1984) covered by our study, will, we believe, bring out significant findings that will be valuable to the investing public as well as to finance and management analysts. Actually, Peters and Waterman's study falls in the same genre as *Fortune* magazine's study of the largest firms or "most-admired" firms. In that respect the study of the excellent firms is as relevant as the role of the largest 108 firms that are shaping our economy today. Our primary aim is to study the financial performance of these companies and not managerial performance as such.

More important, this is the first time that a variety of analytical tools has been used to examine the financial performance of these firms. We have developed a financial analysis framework to seek the answer to whether these so-called "excellent" companies were excellent from management's as well as from the stockholders' point of view. We believe that the analysis demonstrates both the transitory values of excellence and the management bias inherent in the work of Peters and Waterman. Our study, by bringing these analytical tools to bear on the topic of excellence, will add knowledge to the discipline and answer the questions of whether these firms were truly excellent, what their current status is, and what the future will hold for them.

# Redefining Excellence

# 1

# Introduction

Thomas J. Peters and Robert H. Waterman, Jr.'s book *In Search of Excellence* drew wide attention and created quite a stir in business and academic circles when it first appeared in October 1982. Since then it has become a perennial best seller among business publications.[1] In their study, the authors listed sixty-two U.S. companies that they considered innovative and "excellent" firms that seemed to make special efforts to foster, nourish, and care for the products they sell and the people they cater to as their customers or employees. Peters and Waterman discussed eight attributes that distinguish these "excellent" companies in the United States from others. They examined six measures of growth of assets and equities, as well as the returns on capital, equities, and sales, to find out which among these sixty-two firms passed all the tests to become truly "excellent" during 1961–1980, the time period covered by their study.

The book received lavish praise and enthusiastic accolades in business journals and general periodical literature, particularly for its central theme that U.S. companies can regain their competitive edge in the domestic as well as the world markets by paying attention to people—customers and employees—and by sticking to the skills and values they know best. [2] This view caught the public imagination because it portrayed the product champions as "heroes" believing so strongly in their ideas as to take it on themselves to cut through bureaucracy and maneuver their projects through the system and out to the customer. Their view touched a sympathetic chord when the authors emphasized the deficiencies of the narrow, mechanistic short-term approach to decision-making processes as opposed to benefits of planning in accord with the long-term *values* of the organization. In 1982, their clarion call of "productivity through people" seemed to promise a panacea that would solve the multitude of problems for U.S. companies, and bring back the glory days of the 1960s and early 1970s, when Europe and other countries were digging in against the onslaught of what Jean-Jaques Servan-Schreiber called, in his book by that name, *The American Challenge*.[3]

There were many critics, however, who were quick to point out the inherent shortcomings of the study. *Business Week* epitomized the general tenor of criticism leveled by most of the business periodicals, when, in a cover story titled "Who's Excellent Now?," it asked the crucial questions: Were these companies excellent in the first place? Are the eight attributes of excellence described by Peters and Waterman the *only* eight attributes of excellence? Does adhering to them make a difference?[4] The magazine undertook a follow-up study of the forty-three excellent firms and found that at least fourteen of the forty-three companies highlighted by Peters and Waterman had lost their luster within just two years. It cited the cases of Revlon, Atari, Avon, and a few other firms that should never have made anybody's list of well-managed companies because they were characterized by out-of-control management, bloated fiefdoms, and a lack of inward focus. The magazine pinpointed the obvious problem with this kind of study: that the excellent firms of today may not necessarily be the excellent firms of tomorrow.

The book also drew wide criticism in the professional journals. In the *Harvard Business Review,* Daniel T. Carroll called it "a disappointing search for excellence," and criticized the book for ignoring the importance of such factors as proprietary technology, market dominance, control of critical raw materials, government policy, and national culture.[5] He pointed out that even the most strict adherence of Peters and Waterman's eight attributes would not permit IBM to succeed for very long unless it had innovative and protected technology, and that oil companies such as Exxon or Atlantic Richfield would suffer without access to lower-cost supplies, no matter how well they implemented the eight attributes. Moreover, management excellence alone cannot be expected to restore a work ethic to a nation like the United States, enabling U.S. companies to compete on this score with counterparts in Japan. Peters and Waterman's book is disappointing also because of the absence of any serious description of how the excellent companies were analyzed. Apart from occasional references to financial analyses, the only supporting evidence Peters and Waterman offer is a series of anecdotes about the companies and quotations from their leaders. To Carroll, the authors missed the opportunity to build a formalistic "new management theory" as compared to the now-existing rational model taught at the business schools. Furthermore, the authors' view is misconceived because non-management variables such as technology, finance, government policy, and raw materials are not taken into account.

In the *Financial Analysts' Journal*, Michelle Clayman took up Peters and Waterman's sample of the excellent companies and analyzed them empirically to see how well these companies performed in the three years following the publication of the book.[6] She examined twenty-nine excellent companies and found that their financial health had begun to deteriorate almost immediately after the date on which they were selected as excellent. Using the same financial measures as Peters and Waterman did, Clayman found that between 1981 and 1985, as compared to 1976–1980, twenty-five companies (86%) experienced decline in asset growth rate, and twenty-seven (93%) had a fall in equity growth rate; twenty companies (69%) showed a drop in market-to-book ratio, and twenty-four companies (83%) had lower average returns on total capital. Her calculations indicated that twenty-three companies (79%) also had lower average returns on equity, and twenty-four firms (83%) had lower average returns on sales. Thus, her analysis suggests that companies presently achieving excellent results will tend to experience more average outcomes in the future, conforming to the role of "reversion to the mean." That is, over time, distinctive properties of members of a group tend to converge to the average value for the group as a whole.

In order to compare the portfolio returns of these twenty-nine excellent companies, Clayman selected thirty-nine "unexcellent" companies that belong to the cohort that comprises Standard & Poor's 500 stock index, and that had (at the end of 1980) the worst combination of the six financial characteristics. Between 1981 and 1985, the portfolio of the twenty-nine excellent companies wound up with eighteen underperformers and eleven outperformers. It beat Standard & Poor's 500 stock index by 1 percent per year. The portfolio of the unexcellent companies resulted in twenty-five outperformers and fourteen underperformers. It beat Standard & Poor's 500 stock index by over 12 percent per year. Both portfolios had almost identical betas and standard deviations. The beta of the excellent portfolio was 1.18, and its annual standard deviation was 17.7 percent, while the unexcellent portfolio had a beta of 1.17, and its annual standard deviation was 18 percent. The unexcellent portfolio, however, had a monthly alpha or non-market return of 1.0 percent, while the excellent portfolio's monthly alpha value was only 0.2 percent. Clayman inferred from her analysis that the "good" companies underperform because the market overstates their future growth and future return on equity, and as a result, their market-to-book ratios of stocks are overvalued. The converse would be true for the "poor" companies.

Our basic criticisms of Peters and Waterman's approach to studying the excellent firms are more fundamental and methodological in nature. To begin with, when we analyze performance over a longer period of time, there is no such thing as an excellent firm. Firms deemed excellent at one point in time generally find it hard to maintain that lofty position in the future. By the very nature of the inherent dynamics of the economy, excellent firms are subject to the same competitive and other market forces as the non-excellent firms, and are likely to be toppled from that pantheon in a fairly short time. With changes in such factors as product designs, consumer preferences, management turnover, and international competition, firms are under constant pressure to keep their market share from shrinking. Even so-called excellent firms are not immune to a wave of takeovers and other corporate restructuring such as we witnessed during the 1980s. During this decade, for instance, quite a few excellent firms have been swallowed up by non-excellent firms with tremendous liquid assets.

Moreover, the Efficient Market Hypotheses (EMH) of the finance literature asserts that in a world of perfect mobility and knowledge, no individual or firm has a monopoly on information, and the market discounts information in such a way that the shareholders of any firm, excellent or not, will not reap any above-average returns on a long-term basis. In a risk-return world of reality, the returns are commensurate with risks, and any long-run, above-average returns are the result of undertaking abnormal risks. Following the tenets of the EMH, we would expect, then, that the excellent firms on Peters and Waterman's list will not enjoy any superior returns for their shareholders as compared to the non-excellent firms, given similar risk situations.

Furthermore, the excellent firms also belong to their respective industries, which go through the product life cycles of pioneering, stability, maturity, and decline. A firm that is excellent at the growing stage of the industry, will, in general, find it very difficult to remain excellent when that industry moves into maturity or slides into decline. No one would call the USX Corporation an excellent firm today. Some twenty years ago, however, its original, United States Steel Corporation, was one of the dominant firms in the U.S. economy. Following the measures employed by

Peters and Waterman, it was an excellent firm in the 1960s. But with the recent decline of the entire steel industry, it too has declined. For the same reason, many firms belonging to the so-called smokestack industries have lost their glory and fallen on bad times. Because of relative economic decline, excellent companies such as Blue Bell or Levi Strauss had to privatize to prevent being taken over by other companies. The same will be true in the future for many firms listed as excellent in Peters and Waterman's book.

Finally, when we take the size-mobility of firms into account, we find that in any list of excellent firms, largest firms, or most admired firms, a significant percentage of them will disappear from that list over time. Large firms or excellent firms do not enjoy any secure entrenchment by virtue of their size or managerial excellence. They will always face strong direct competition from their rivals in the same industry, or from those moving into those industries. In his historic study of the big enterprises in the United States, A. D. H. Kaplan found that of the largest 100 industrial firms in 1909, only fifty-three remained in that list after ten years, and only thirty-six of them stayed among the 100 in 1948.[7] This tendency is more pronounced today when the size-mobility of firms has increased significantly in comparison to past decades. Following Gibrat's Law of proportionate effect, Edwin Mansfield argues that, over time, the surviving smaller firms tend to have higher and more variable growth rates than the larger firms.[8] Since Peters and Waterman take the growth rates of assets, sales, and equities as their main quantitative criteria for the selection of the excellent firms, Gibrat's Law predicts that many of the existing excellent firms will be eclipsed in the course of time. Relatively smaller firms will emerge as excellent in the future because they have the potential for growth. Thus the listing of a group of firms by any label at any point of time has little economic significance, particularly in the context of size-mobility and the dynamics of firm growth.

Essentially, Peters and Waterman's study of the U.S. excellent firms falls in the same genre as Professor Early's pioneering study of the "excellently managed" companies done in 1956.[9] A. D. H. Kaplan's study of the largest U.S. industrial enterprises and Collins and Preston's study of the 100 largest U.S. manufacturing firms also fall in to the same category.[10] Since 1983, *Fortune* magazine has started to analyze America's "most admired" corporations.[11] The fundamental problem with this kind of study is that it is biased toward the largest corporations in the industries concerned. All these studies focus on firms that are among the largest in their respective industries and enjoy a dominant market share at the time of analysis. But many not-so-big firms could also be excellent in terms of other attributes described by Peters and Waterman. Although they chose to include a few relatively smaller firms in their study, it is important to note that forty-two out of the fifty-four public companies, or about 80 percent of the total public corporations in their list of excellent firms, were included in *Fortune*'s directory of the 500 largest U.S. industrial companies in 1985.[12]

The main purpose of this book is to analyze, in the financial analysis framework, those firms listed in Peters and Waterman's book as the sample of excellent firms, covering the same period as they did, and bringing the analysis up to date. While Peters and Waterman did analyze these firms using the tools of financial analysis, the main thrust of their approach was to gauge the managerial performance of these firms. They were seeking to discover if these excellent firms were excellent from the management's point of view, if the managers of these firms were "product champions," and if these firms were achieving what the authors called "productivity through people." Nowhere in this book did they ask if the stockholders of the companies enjoyed above-average returns for any duration of time. Moreover, Peters and Waterman surprisingly dismissed favorable shareholders' returns (i.e., investment performance) as a characteristic of managerial excellence.[13]

Our main approach, in contrast, is to ask if the excellent firms are excellent from the stockholders' point of view. As the stockholders are the true owners of public companies, it is of paramount importance to them to determine if they reap any above-average returns by being the shareholders of these excellent firms, and if they gain any pecuniary benefits from acquisitions, divestitures, or other restructurings of these excellent firms. Since our main concern is the nature and extent of returns to the stockholders, not to the management alone, Agency Theory is crucial to our analysis.[14] It is a tenet of this theory that because of the separation of ownership and management of the public corporations, there may be a divergence between the interests of the stockholders and the management. The managers of a public company may not keep the interests of the shareholders foremost in their minds. From the stockholders' point of view, for a firm to be a truly excellent firm, the management must strive to maximize the value of the firm (the value of the stockholders' equity) over the long run. Any analysis that does not take this view significantly into account is of little use to the actual or putative owners of such firms. In fact, such analysis may be positively harmful to their interests, a situation this book attempts to remedy. One way of stating our review of the question of excellence here is to say that we reopen it by asking: Excellent for whom? For how long? With what benefits to the shareholders?

## A CRITICAL REVIEW OF PETERS AND WATERMAN'S STUDY OF THE UNITED STATES' EXCELLENT FIRMS

At the very outset of their study (chapter 1), Peters and Waterman delineate the eight attributes that characterize the distinction of the excellent firms. They are: (1) a bias for action; (2) close proximity to the customer; (3) autonomy and entrepreneurship; (4) productivity through people; (5) a hands-on, value-driven philosophy; (6) "stick to the knitting" philosophy; (7) "simple form, lean staff"; and (8) simultaneous loose–tight properties. None of these eight attributes is startling, as the authors point out, and some, if not most, are "motherhoods." Yet almost no one really lives by them. It is the vigorous implementation of them that supposedly makes good companies excellent.

Peters and Waterman group their sample of sixty-two companies into the following six industry groupings: (1) high-technology companies, such as Digital Equipment, Hewlett-Packard, Intel, and Texas Instruments; (2) consumer goods companies, such as Procter and Gamble, Chesebrough-Pond's, and Johnson & Johnson; (3) general industrial goods companies, which included Caterpillar Tractor, Dana Corporation, and 3M; (4) service companies such as Delta Airlines, Marriott, McDonald's, and Disney Productions; (5) project management companies such as Bechtel and Fluor; and (6) resource-based companies such as Atlantic Richfield, Dow Chemical, and Exxon. They do not include in their sample any banking or financial institutions, and they leave out most chemical and drug companies. Nor do they include any foreign companies doing business in the United States. Since their major concern is to probe how big companies stay "alive, well and innovative," they do not look extensively at companies whose sales were less than $1 billion during the period covered by their study. A full list of these companies is given in table 1.1, along with the indication of which of them pass all the tests of excellence.

The authors calculate the following six measures of the long-term superiority of these firms over a twenty-year period, from 1961 to 1980: (1) compound asset growth (a "least square" measure that fits a curve to annual growth data); (2) compound equity growth (a "least square" measure of annual growth data); (3) the averge ratio of market-to-book value of common stocks (measuring "wealth creation"); (4) average return on total capital; (5) average return on equity; and (6) average return on sales. In order to qualify as a top performer, a company must have been in the top half of its industry in at least four out of six of these measures

**Table 1.1**

**Names of the Excellent Firms Listed in Peters and Waterman's Book**

Structured Interviews Plus 25-Year Literature Review

| High Technology | Consumer Goods | General Industrial |
|---|---|---|
| Allen-Bradley** | Blue Bell | Caterpillar Tractor* |
| Amdahl* | Eastman Kodak* | Dana Corporation* |
| Digital Equipment* | Frito-L (Pepsi Co)** | Ingersoll-Rand |
| Emerson Electric* | General Foods | McDermott |
| Gould | Johnson & Johnson* | Minnesota Mining & |
| Hewlett-Packard* | Procter & Gamble* |  Manufacturing* |
| International Business Machines* | | |
| National Cash Register | | |
| Rockwell | **Service** | **Project Management** |
| Schlumberger* | Delta Airlines* | Bechtel** |
| Texas Instruments* | Marriott* | Boeing* |
| United Technologies | McDonalds'* | Fluor* |
| Western Electric | | |
| Westinghouse | **Resource-Based** | |
| Xerox | Exxon | |

Limited Interviews Plus 25-Year Literature Review

| High Technology | Consumer Goods | General Industrial |
|---|---|---|
| Data General* | Atari (Warner Com- | General Motors |
| General Electric |  munications)** | |
| Hughes Aircraft** | Avon* | |
| Intel* | Bristol-Myers* | |
| Lockheed | Chesebrough-Pond's* | |
| National Semiconductor* | Levi Strauss* | |
| Raychem* | Mars** | |
| TRW | Maytag* | |
| Wang Labs* | Merck* | |
| | Polaroid | |
| | Revlon* | |
| | Tupperware (Dart & | |
| |  Krafts)** | |

| Service | Project Management | Resource-Based |
|---|---|---|
| American Airlines | | Arco |
| Disney Productions* | | Dow Chemical* |
| K-Mart* | | Du Pont* |
| Wal-Mart* | | Standard Oil (Indiana)/ |
| | |  Amoco* |

** Privately held or subsidiary; no extensive public data available,
   but estimated to pass all hurdles for "excellent" performance.

* Passes all hurdles for "excellent" performance, 1961-1980.

Source: Thomas J. Peters and Robert H. Waterman, In Search of
        Excellence: Lessons from America's Best Run Companies.
        Reprinted by permission; (c) 1982 by Harper & Row,
        Publishers, Inc.

over the full twenty-year period. As a last test, they applied a measure of innovativeness per se, as they asked selected questions to industry experts (e.g., businesspeople from within the industry) to rate the companies' twenty-year records of innovation, defined as ''a continuous flow of industry bellwether products and services and general rapidness of response to changing markets or other external dynamics."[15]

Out of their list of sixty-two companies, forty-three passed all the tests. Of these they report that they interviewed twenty-one companies in depth, while conducting less extensive interviews in each of the remaining twenty-two firms. They also report that they interviewed twelve companies that just barely missed the passing grade. Furthermore, they examined a group of companies they called "Exemplars," which, without benefit of specific selection criteria, do seem to represent especially well both sound performance and the eight traits they had identified. (These companies include Johnson & Johnson, Procter & Gamble, 3M, and eleven others.) The authors seem firmly to believe that the excellent companies achieved excellence because of a unique set of cultural attributes that distinguishes them from the rest.

Peters and Waterman's aim is to criticize the so-called rational model (chapter 2) taught at the graduate schools of business and practiced by the alumni of these schools. The main architects of this numerative, rationalistic approach to management were Harold Geneen, former chairman of ITT, and Robert McNamara, former president of Ford Motor Company and secretary of defense for the United States. The rational model seeks detached, analytical justification for all managerial decisions, and teaches us that well-trained professional managers can manage anything. To Peters and Waterman, the rational model emphasizes analysis that is too complex to be useful and too unwieldy to be flexible, analysis that strives to be precise about the inherently unpredictable—such as detailed market forecasts when the end use of a new product is still hazy. Here planning becomes an end in itself. The plan itself becomes the truth, and data that do not fit the preconceived plan are denigrated or ignored. The rational model treats people as factors of production, while cost reduction becomes the chief priority and revenue enhancement is underemphasized. It propels us to an abstract, heartless philosophy that does not value experimentation and abhors mistakes. The rational model leads us inevitably to overcomplexity and inflexibility.

In place of the rational model, Peters and Waterman try to create an eclectic "New Theory" (chapters 3 and 4) of excellent organization in which B. F. Skinner's theory of positive reinforcement is pursued vigorously (where both simplicity and the complexity of the tasks are performed in a balanced way); shared values or cultures are nurtured; and "transforming leadership" (i.e., leadership that builds on human's need for meaning, leadership that creates institutional purpose) occurs in such a way that leaders and followers raise one another to higher levels of motivation and morality. In other words, the management of an excellent company creates environments in which people can flourish, develop self-esteem, and otherwise become excited participants in the business and in society as a whole. Peters and Waterman talk of the four stages in the history of the theory of organization and management: the closed system–rational actor era espoused by Max Weber and Frederick Taylor; the closed system–social era described by Elton Mayo, Chester Barnard and others; the open system–rational actor era developed mainly by Alfred Chandler; and the more recent open system–social actor era postulated by Karl Weick and James March. Peters and Waterman lay the groundwork of the New Theory, which would include the basic human needs in organization—(1) people's need for meaning; (2) people's need for a modicum of control; (3) people's need for positive reinforcement—and the degree to which actions and behaviors shape attitudes and beliefs rather than vice versa. Their theory also stresses the notion of companies, especially the excellent ones, as having distinctive cultures; and the emergence of the successful companies through purposeful, but specifically unpredictable, evolution. The rest of the book (chapters 5 through 12) is devoted to the authors' espousal of eight attributes, which are to be woven into the New Theory. One chapter is allotted for each attribute, described in detail through interviews with the management of these companies as well as with quotations from books and journals supporting their position.

There are, however, some serious shortcomings in Peters and Waterman's study of the United States' excellent firms. First, the whole approach of the book is more anecdotal than analytical. Although they try to formulate a New Theory of organizational behavior, it is essentially an amorphous, loosely knit jumble of ideas, not a theoretical model that can be the basis of empirical and quantitative investigations of the excellent firms. As a matter of fact, the authors themselves admit that it is in a "fairly early and messy stage of development," and "largely obscure, tied to the 'real world' only by implication," because it is a "leading-edge theory."[16] Thus, Peters and Waterman do not present any well-structured theory, but talk of the eight attributes and the common linkages observed among the excellent companies. Obviously, this cannot be construed as a full-fledged theory.

Second, Peters and Waterman's study is devoid of any statistical tables, figures, or charts. While the authors talk of undertaking six measures of excellent firms, they do not present their findings in any statistical tables for the readers to judge. Out of the sixty-two firms, they find forty-three to be truly excellent. But were they truly excellent throughout the two decades (1961-1980) covered by their study? Would they have been excellent if the time period were 1965-1975, or some other interval? How did these firms behave during the bull market of 1963-1967, and in the bear market of 1974-1975, or during the periods of high inflation and deep recession we have witnessed during the last two decades? The book is silent about the impact of business cycles or other economic and financial forces influencing the outcomes by which an excellent firm is judged. We have to take their word that the firms selected are excellent, for no numerical evidence is adduced to support that claim. The authors rely too much on secondary sources.

Third, Peters and Waterman's use of industrial groupings or categories is highly unsatisfactory and theoretically objectionable. They do not follow any Standard Industrial Classifications (SIC) codes of two-, three-, or four-digit industry classifications. Instead, they form industrial categories based on popular concepts such as "high technology," "consumer goods," or "general industrial goods companies," which they themselves admit are ill-defined. Following these criteria, they group together firms that belong to entirely different four-digit industry classifications. Even with respect to the two-digit industry codes, issued by the U.S. Office of Management and Budget and used by the Federal Statistical Policy and Standards Office, they differ. Thus, in the high technology grouping, they include computer companies such as Amdahl, Digital Equipment, and IBM (Code No. 44), but also United Technologies (No. 41), and Westinghouse (No. 36). Similarly, in the consumer goods category, they include Blue Bell (No. 23) and General Foods (No. 20), but also Bristol-Myers (No. 42), and Revlon (No. 43). In no categories do they include firms that all belong to the same lines of business, except in the broadest sense of the term. This makes their discussion of whether any company is excellent in any particular industry or sector superfluous and downright erroneous.

Fourth, Peters and Waterman ignore the stockholders' point of view when discussing the excellent firms. They rely mainly on the managerial expertise as the determinant of excellence. According to their definition, excellence consists of three main attributes: (1) continuous innovation, (2) large size, and (3) sustained financial performance over the twenty-year period (1961-1980). But they dismiss any favorable shareholder returns as a characteristic of firm excellence. Since the stockholders of the public companies are the true owners of these enterprises, it is important to consider whether these companies maximize their shareholders' returns in the long run (i.e., whether the managers enhance the values of their respective firms more than the non-excellent firms). We all know that if the increase in earnings per share or any such financial improvements are not reflected in the long-term increase in the values of the companies concerned, then sooner or later those companies will be up for grabs and will be subject to takeover bids or other restructuring, as we witness so frequently in the economy today.

Finally, as was pointed out earlier, excellence is more related to a point in time than to a long period; it would be very hard, if not impossible, for a firm to maintain excellence for a prolonged period of time, not to mention two decades. Even by the end of the period of Peters and Waterman study, some of the luster of the so-called excellent firms had vanished. Thus, although Dana Corporation had performed well in the earlier part of the period, its heavy reliance on automotive and truck business has damaged its more recent performance. Similarly, Boeing's market share in the commercial jet market has declined of late. Texas Instruments' failure in digital watch and pocket calculators is too well known to recite in detail. Quite a few companies named in the list of Peters and Waterman's excellent companies, compiled in 1980, would look less attractive in 1988. Companies such as Schlumberger, Fluor, and Caterpillar Tractor have seen their fortunes tumble with the shrinkage of their respective industries. Companies such as Texas Instruments, National Semiconductor, Intel, and Wang Laboratories have had to undergo extensive changes, abandoning some of their businesses and markets. Finally, companies such as Avon and Eastman Kodak found their primary products and delivery systems outmoded soon after 1980.

In Table 1.2, we have listed the disappearance, by 1987, of some of the well-known publicly held excellent firms.

This table shows that in spite of receiving a clean bill of corporate health from Peters and Waterman, these giant firms and leaders of their respective industries became victims of takeovers by other non-excellent firms. This is because of the rather lackluster performances of these excellent firms during recent years, when their financial performance came into further scrutiny in a bullish and vigorous stock market.


## PRIOR STUDIES OF EXCELLENT FIRMS

Peters and Waterman's analysis was not the first one about the excellent firms in the United States. Long before their study appeared, Professor James Early had attempted to analyze the marginal policies of the "excellently-managed" companies. He took the names of the excellent

**Table 1.2**
**Disappearance of the Publicly Held Excellent Firms by 1987**

| Name of the Firm | Reasons for Disappearance |
|---|---|
| Blue Bell | Privately held in Dec. 1984 |
| Chesebrough-Pond's* | Acquired by Unilever United States, Inc. in Feb. 1987 |
| General Foods | Acquired by Philip Morris, Inc. on Nov. 1, 1985 |
| Levi Strauss* | Acquired by HHF Corp.in August 1985 |

*According to Peters and Waterman, these firms passed all

hurdles for excellent performance during 1961-1980.

Source: Moody's Industrial Manuals, covering 1984-1987.

firms from the *Manual of Excellent Managements*, published by the American Institute of Management.[17] The 1954 *Manual* listed 348 excellently managed companies, of which 217 were considered to be primarily in manufacturing. Early's survey was confined to the 100 companies that responded to his questionnaire. These were all leading firms, presumably in the vanguard regarding the use of newer management techniques. They were all fairly large companies, with median assets of $50 to $100 million, and median sales in the $100 to $250 million range in 1954.

Early found that short views, innovative sensitivity, marginal costing, and marginal pricing were all preponderant among the responding companies. But the companies' short-range policies were consistent with their long-range costing, pricing, and other product-related policies. The majority of these excellently managed companies did not view short-run vs. long-run profitability as alternative and inconsistent goals. Rather, they sought to maximize their long-run welfare by alertly trying to maintain and increase their current profits within their practicable horizons. Almost all of them followed marginal cost and accounting principles to enhance their short- and long-term performances.

Early did not agree with Professor Herbert Simon's claim that the goal of the majority of firms was to obtain "satisficing profits" rather than to maximize profits, as postulated in economics and finance literature.[18] On the contrary, he found that a striking characteristic of the excellently managed firms was their systematic focus upon cost reduction, the expansion of revenue, and the increase of profits. These firms strove always to be better, and frequently to be the best, not just good. He found that the major objectives of the excellent firms were high managerial incomes, good profits, a strong competitive position, and growth. The tendency towards profit maximization (i.e., highest practicable profits) was the outgrowth of the need for internal financing to expand the firms, as they were extremely reluctant to grow by merger. This contradicted the study of Professor Weston, done at the same time, which found that 22.6 percent of the growth of large firms in the United States was due to mergers and acquisitions.[19]

While Early's pioneering study focused on the goals and practices of the excellently managed firms, A. D. H. Kaplan focused on the 100 largest manufacturing firms in the United States, examining their turnovers and domination in their respective industries from 1909 to 1948.[20] As mentioned before, he found that of the 100 largest firms in the United States in 1909, only 36 survived in that list in 1948. In addition, of the 100 largest firms in 1919, only 26 remained on the list in 1948.

The list for 1919 showed 47 firms that replaced the firms in the largest 100 list in 1909. In 1929, of the 53 original companies that were still among the largest 100 firms in 1919, 16 firms had failed to maintain their places after only a decade. Among the companies on the 1948 list only 36 remained, disregarding the change of names; of the remaining 64, 25 appeared first in 1919, 14 in 1929, 5 in 1935, and only 20 in 1948. This showed a tremendous turnover among the largest firms, and the fact that the largest firms, many of which became excellent firms in Peters and Waterman's list, did not enjoy any security of position by virtue of their size, nor were they immune from severe competition from their business rivals.

In 1983, *Fortune* magazine started to publish a list of America's most admired corporations.[21] Generally, the magazine would poll more than 8,000 top executives, outside directors, and financial analysts, and would assign points on a scale of 0 (poor) to 10 (excellent) among roughly 300 companies from *Fortune*'s list of 500 largest industrial and 500 largest service companies. As if taking the cue from Peters and Waterman's book, the magazine also talked of eight attributes or measures by which the ranking would be made. These are: quality of management, quality of products or services, innovativeness, long-term investment value, financial soundness, community and enviromental responsibility, use of corporate assets, and ability to attract, develop, and keep talented people. It is interesting to note that *Fortune* has included three financial criteria in its eight attributes, while Peters and Waterman had one in their list.

In order to compare the list of *Fortune*'s ten best or excellent companies with Peters and Waterman's list, and to see the nature of turnover, we have listed, in table 1.3, the ten most admired (excellent) firms in January 1984 and January 1988.

In 1984, six out of these ten firms were included in Peters and Waterman's list of excellent firms, while in 1988 only four excellent firms remained in the most admired list of *Fortune* magazine. Interestingly, five of the six firms that were in the list in 1984 were dropped from it within just four years. Only Merck remained in the 1988 from the original list. IBM, which was number 1 in four consecutive years, fell to the number 8 position in 1987, and was down to number 32 in 1988. This shows again that the excellent or most admired firms meet the same severe competition from their rivals as the non-excellent firms, and their chance of maintaining relative primacy is the same as the non-excellent ones.

## DATA BASE AND PLAN OF THE PRESENT STUDY

Since the main purpose of this study is to examine, from the stockholders' point of view, the United States' excellent firms listed in Peters and Waterman's *In Search of Excellence*, we will be analyzing these firms within the framework of financial analysis. In order to do that, we will not only calculate the growth of assets, sales, and earnings of the firms over time, but also the financial ratios and the capital structure of both the excellent firms and the comparable control or nonexcellent firms for the same period. Since we are more interested in the risk-adjusted returns of the excellent and control firms than their simple returns, we will calculate their beta values for gauging the portfolio risks of the firms, as expounded by William Sharpe and others in the Capital Asset Pricing Model (CAPM).[22] The financial performance of these firms will be measured by forming portfolios, and then comparing them with the portfolios of the control firms by using the familiar Treynor-Sharpe-Jensen portfolio measures.[23]

As noted earlier, one of the important shortcomings of Peters and Waterman's selection of industrial categories is that they do not follow the usual four-digit SIC codes, using ill-defined popular groupings instead. Since we want to compare the financial performances of the excellent firms with the control firms, we have no choice but to abide by their selection of industrial groupings. We have, however, matched their companies with the control firms in the same four-digit codes, wherever possible, and we have matched firms according to size. The full list of the control firms is given in table 1.4.

**Table 1.3**
*Fortune* **Magazine's List of Ten Most-Admired (Excellent) Firms**

| Rank | Company | Industry | Score |
|------|---------|----------|-------|
| | | January, 1984 | |
| 1 | IBM* | Office Equipment & Computers | 8.53 |
| 2 | Dow-Jones | Publishing-Printing | 8.35 |
| 3 | Hewlett-Packard* | Office Equipment & Computers | 8.24 |
| 4 | Merck* | Pharmaceuticals | 8.17 |
| 5 | Johnson & Johnson* | Pharmaceuticals | 8.15 |
| 6 | Time, Inc. | Publishing-Printing | 7.99 |
| 7 | General Electric* | Electronics, Appliances | 7.96 |
| 8 | Anheuser-Busch | Beverages | 7.91 |
| 9 | Coca-Cola | Beverages | 7.87 |
| 10 | Boeing* | Aerospace | 7.79 |
| | | January, 1988 | |
| 1 | Merck* | Pharmaceuticals | 9.00 |
| 2 | Rubbermaid | Rubber Products | 8.29 |
| 3 | Dow Jones | Publishing-Printing | 8.24 |
| 4 | Procter & Gamble* | Soaps, Cosmetics | 8.15 |
| 5 | Liz Claiborne | Apparel | 8.14 |
| 6 | 3M* | Scientific/Photographic Equipment | 8.10 |
| 7 | Philip Morris | Tobacco | 8.07 |
| 8 | J.P. Morgan & Co. | Commercial Banking | 8.03 |
| 9 | RJR Nabisco | Tobacco | 7.90 |
| 10 | Wal-Mart* | Retailing | 7.90 |

* Excellent firms in Peters and Waterman's list.

Source: Fortune, January issues of 1984 and 1988.

**Table 1.4**
**List of the Control Firms—Full Sample**

| High Technology | Consumer Goods | General Industrial |
|---|---|---|
| Bell & Howell | Borden | Armco, Inc. |
| Bell Industries | Coca-Cola | Baker Intern. |
| Burroughs | Kellogg | Ford Motor Co. |
| Harris Corp. | Warner-Lambert | Tenneco |
| RCA Corp. | Kroger Co. | Borg-Warner |
| Singer Co. | American Brands | Cabot Corp. |
| Control Data | American Home Prod. | |
| Sperry Corp. | Colgate-Palmolive | |
| Eaton Corp. | United Brands | |
| Johnson Controls | General Mills | |
| Foxboro Corp. | Pfizer | |
| Honeywell | Philip Morris | |
| ITT | | |
| Motorola | | |
| FMC Corp. | | |
| Tandy Corp. | | |
| Textron | | |
| Zenith | | |
| Fairchild Industries | | |
| Raytheon | | |

| Service | Project Management | Resource-Based |
|---|---|---|
| United Airlines | Grumman | Mobil |
| TWA | Martin Marietta | Chevron |
| Sears | | Occidental Petroleum |
| Federated Dept. Stores | | Allied Corp. |
| J.C. Penney | | Monsanto |
| Pillsbury | | |
| Walgreen | | |

The financial information on both the excellent and control firms is derived from various issues (1960–1984) of Moody's *Industrial Manuals*, Moody's *Transportation Manuals*, and Value Line *Investment Survey*.[24] The acquisitions and divestiture dates are based on relevant volumes of the *Wall Street Journal Index*. If merger or sell-off announcements were not in the *Index*, they were deemed insignificant and were omitted.[25] Also, we could not obtain the relevant financial data on the seven private companies (or subsidiaries of larger corporations about which separate information was not provided) in Peters and Waterman's list of excellent firms. The data on managerial compensation was collected from the proxy statements that companies filed with the Securities and Exchange Commission. The Standard & Poor Index of 500 common stocks was also used whenever necessary as the standard against which the performances of both the excellent and the control firms might be measured.

Stock price and stock return data were obtained from the tapes of the Center for Research in Security Prices (CRSP) at the University of

Chicago.[26] Here the stock returns are calculated by adding dividends to the capital gains (or capital losses) of the firms. An equally weighted index of returns of all the stocks listed in the New York Stock Exchange was taken as a surrogate for the market index. The CRSP tapes now contain both the monthly stock returns and the daily stock returns data. We have taken the monthly returns data because we are going to measure the excellence of our sample firms; monthly data would suit our purposes better, since excellence is a long-term phenomenon (that is, one achieves excellence only after pursuing it for a long time). The daily stock returns data, though useful as a gauge of immediate impact of any important announcements of a firm, would not be very appropriate for our analysis, in which the long-term impact on returns was taken as a measure of excellence.

Peters and Waterman took 1961 to 1980 as the time period for their study of excellent firms. Since we are comparing them with our matching control firms, we have taken 1960 to 1984, in order to bring them up to date. We have also divided these twenty-five years into five-year and ten-year intervals whenever our analysis called for it. For the calculation of the beta values or the systematic risks of the stocks, we have used four types of holding periods: (1) twenty-five one-year periods, with the first beginning January 1, 1960, and the last beginning January 1, 1984; (2) five non-overlapping five-year periods, with the first beginning January 1, 1960, and the last beginning January 1, 1980; (3) four overlapping ten-year periods, with the first beginning January 1, 1960, and ending December 31, 1969, and the last beginning January 1, 1975, and ending December 31, 1984; and (4) the entire twenty-five-year period beginning January 1, 1960, and ending December 31, 1984.

The principle reason why we do not extend the time period beyond 1984 is that we want to compare the data on Peters and Waterman's firms with that of our control firms. Since we are interested to find out whether the so-called excellent firms are truly excellent as compared to the non-excellent or control firms, the appropriate step is to confine our time period as closely as possible to their time period, so that the results are not biased unduly by the latest events taking place in these companies. This is particularly true if we extend the period beyond 1984, when the bull market of the securities was raging and when most common stocks were very much overvalued. Since any comparison of the two sets of data should be done in a relative calm and stable time period, we have sought to make our period of comparison compatible with the period of initial study. However, we have extended the analysis beyond 1984 whenever our study has warranted.

Our study has been divided into six parts. Chapter two examines the performances of the excellent firms as compared to the nonexcellent control firms with respect to sales and asset growth, earnings growth, and returns to the stockholders during 1960–1984. This chapter also places these two groups of firms into two portfolios and compares their risk-adjusted returns, using the Treynor-Sharpe-Jensen measures of portfolio performances. In chapter three, we have calculated the various types of financial ratios of both the excellent and control firms, and summarized them in ratio profiles. This chapter focuses on the operating efficiency of these two groups of firms in selected time intervals.

Chapter four deals with the capital structure characteristics of both the excellent and control firms, such as debt-asset ratios, debt-equity ratios, and the effects of leverage on firm performance, particularly under the assumption of optimal capital structure. Here again, the impact of capital structure on the stock prices as well as the price-earnings ratios has been highlighted. Chapter five discusses the effects of mergers and acquisitions undertaken by the excellent and control firms on their stock returns in the framework of the "event studies," as found in financial literature. Here we have divided our samples into larger versus smaller acquisitions as well as conglomerate versus non-conglomerate acquisitions in order to gauge the impact of these differences on the return statistics. Similarly, in chapter six we have calculated the effects of divestitures of the excellent and control firms on their stock returns. We have divided the total samples into larger versus smaller divestitures, and price disclosure versus non-price disclosure impact on the stock returns. Chapter seven delves into the relationship of executive compensation and stock performance. Here we have tried to correlate the managerial renumerations not only with sales, assets, and earnings growth of the two groups of firms, but also with their risk-adjusted (beta) returns. Finally, in chapter eight, we have drawn the summary and conclusions of the study as a critique of Peters and Waterman's important treatise, *In Search of Excellence*.

Despite many inherent limitations of data source, the financial analysis brings out the strengths or weaknesses of a firm or industry as recorded in its past. The analysis will focus on the long-run trend of the financial ratios and the capital structure, which shapes and molds the performance of the companies over many years. The growth and variability of earnings, assets, and share prices will not only show the uneven records of their performances, but also predict turbulent years lying ahead of them. Since we are interested in the risk-adjusted returns of the stocks as well as the portfolios, the beta analysis will focus on the nature and extent of the systematic (market) risk faced by the investors, apart from the unsystematic (diversifiable) risk inherent in the ownership of any stock. The event study will show the nature and duration of any excess returns earned by the stockholders from the restructuring of the firms, such as through acquisitions or divestitures.

We believe that our analysis is a worthwhile attempt to examine the groups of firms that are vital to the well-being of our economy because of the dominant roles they play in their respective industries. These are the companies that are generally large, growth-oriented, and technologically innovative. Along with the comparable control firms, these hundred-odd companies constitute a very important segment of our national economy. Since our study focuses on the returns to the stockholders, not the management alone, it brings out the implications of modern financial theory. Again, if a firm is truly excellent, not only should it be excellent in terms of its shareholders and managers, but also in comparison to rival firms belonging to the same industry. Without this context, the supposed excellence of a firm is devoid of any long-term economic and financial significance.

## NOTES

1. Thomas J. Peters and Robert H. Waterman, Jr., *In Search of Excellence: Lessons from America's Best Run Companies* (New York: Harper & Row, 1982).

2. Some of the reviews of the book in popular journals: "By the Book," *Time*, Vol. 122 (Oct. 17, 1983):68–69; "Tom Peters and Bob Waterman Searched for Excellence and Created a Business Bible," *People*, Vol. 20 (Dec. 26, 1983):96–97; "Well-Run Companies: The Secret of Success," *U.S. News & World Report*, Vol. 95 (Oct. 10, 1983):74+; "Economics Without Numbers," *Washington Monthly*, Vol. 16 (March 1984):40–46; "Treat People like Winners!" *Reader's Digest*, Vol. 125 (Sept. 1984):96–99; "Excellent by the Hour," *Fortune*, Vol. 110 (Dec. 10, 1984):225+; "The Peter Phenomenon," *Publishers' Weekly*, Vol. 226 (Oct. 26, 1984):101.

3. Jean-Jacques Servan-Schreiber, *The American Challenge* (New York: Atheneum, 1968).

4. "Who's Excellent Now?" *Business Week*, Nov. 5, 1984, 76–88.

5. Daniel T. Carroll, "A Disappointing Search for Excellence," *Harvard Business Review*, Vol. 61 (Dec. 1983):78–88.

6. Michelle Clayman, "In Search of Excellence—The Investor's Viewpoint," *Financial Analysts' Journal* Vol. 43 (May–June 1987):54–63.

7. A. D. H. Kaplan, *Big Enterprise in a Competitive System* (Washington, D.C.: The Brookings Institute, rev. ed., 1964), pp. 135–36.

8. Edwin Mansfield, "Entry, Gibrat's Law, Innovation, and the Growth of Firms," *American Economic Review*, Vol. 52 (December 1962), pp. 1031–46.

9. James Early, "Marginal Policies of Excellently Managed Companies," *American*

10. Norman Collins and Lee Preston, "The Size Structure of the Largest Industrial Firms, 1909-1958" *American Economic Review*, Vol. 51 (Dec. 1961):986-1011.

11. *Fortune*, January 10, 1983, p. 35.

12. *Fortune*, April 29, 1985, pp. 266-85.

13. Peters and Waterman, *In Search of Excellence*, pp. 24-25.

14. Michael Jensen and William Meckling, "Theory of the Firm: Managerial Behavior, Agency Costs and Ownership Structure," *Journal of Financial Economics*, Vol. 3 (March 1976):305-60.

15. Peters and Waterman, *In Search of Excellence*, p. 23.

16. Peters and Waterman, *In Search of Excellence*, pp. 89-118.

17. Early, "Marginal Policies," p. 45.

18. Herbert Simon, "Theories of Decision-Making in Economics and Behavioral Science," *American Economic Review*, Vol. 49 (June 1959):255-81.

19. Fred Weston, *The Role of Mergers in the Growth of Large Firms* (Berkeley: University of California Press, 1953).

20. A. D. H. Kaplan, *Big Enterprise*, pp. 28-39.

21. *Fortune*, Jan. 10, 1983, pp. 34-44.

22. William Sharpe, "Capital Asset Prices: A Theory of Market Equilibrium under Conditions of Risk," *Journal of Finance*, Vol. 19 (Sept. 1964):425-42.

23. Jack Treynor, "How to Rate Management of Investment Funds," *Harvard Business Review*, Vol. 43 (Jan.-Feb. 1965):63-75; William Sharpe, "Mutual Fund Performance," *Journal of Business*, Vol. 39 (Jan. 1966):119-38; Michael Jensen, "The Performance of Mutual Funds in the Period 1945-1964," *Journal of Finance,* Vol. 23 (May 1968):389-416.

24. Moody's *Industrial Manuals*, Moody's *Transportation Manuals*, Value Line *Investment Survey*, various issues covering 1960-1984.

25. *Wall Street Journal Index*, various issues covering 1960-1984.

26. Center for Research in Security Prices (CRSP), University of Chicago; CRSP Tapes covering 1960-1984.

# 2

# Comparative Performance of Excellent Versus Control Firms

Growth is one of the most important measures of corporate performance. A company that is not growing, either by sales or assets, or by earnings, is sure to lose ground against its competitors, and will be subject to future take-over bids or mergers not conducive to its ultimate survival. This is particularly true for the so-called excellent firm, for, by definition, it should be in the forefront of the industry to which it belongs and the general economy of which it is an essential part. Since our main objective is to examine whether the so-called excellent firms were truly excellent and remained so during the past two and a half decades, we would normally expect above-average growth from these firms during the years covered by our study.

In this chapter, we have estimated the growth of assets, sales, and earnings of the excellent firms from 1960 through 1984. Since we are interested in both the absolute and the relative growth rates of these firms, we have also calculated the growth of the control firms in our sample for comparative purposes. Because our main objective is to gauge the financial performance of these firms, we have estimated the growth of earnings per share as well as the price-earning ratios of these firms, and compared them with that of Standard & Poor's index of 500 common stocks—a widely used yardstick of relative stock performance. Furthermore, in order to measure the risk-adjusted returns of these companies, we have also used the familiar Treynor-Sharpe-Jensen indexes to find out whether these firms were truly excellent from the shareholders' point of view.[1]

## ASSETS AND SALES GROWTH OF THE EXCELLENT
## AND CONTROL FIRMS, 1960–1984

In table 2.1, we have calculated the index of assets of the excellent and the control firms from 1960 through 1984, with 1960 as the base year (i.e., 1960 = 100). For the excellent firms, the growth of the index was very impressive indeed for all six groupings of our sample during the twenty-five-year period 1960–1984. Here we find that the firms in the high technology grouping were not the highest in growth of assets. Predominance in the arc of asset growth belonged to firms in the service industry, which grew by a factor of 27 during this period, and which has had the highest growth rate in the general economy during the last two decades.[2] Firms in project management came second in the index of asset growth, while firms in high technology took third place. The least growth of assets was attained by firms in the general industrial and resource-based groupings, slow-growth sectors of the economy as a whole during the last two decades. But the consumer goods sector had an impressive growth of the index in 1984 as compared to 1960; firms in this grouping grew by a factor of 14 in twenty-five years. Again, the index registered the highest growth by firms in the six groupings during the more recent decade, particularly during 1980–1984, when the economy started to pick up speed after the severe recession of 1974–1975 and the rather sluggish growth after that.

When we compare the index of the growth of assets for the excellent firms with that of the control firms, we find that the aggregate index of the latter grew about 80 points higher than the former one during 1960–1984. Here again, the service sector grew most vigorously, followed by the resource-based firms, and then by firms in high technology. The firms in the consumer goods grouping also showed their strength, growing by a factor of 11 times in 1984 as compared to 1960. For most of the firms in the control group, however, the highest of this index occurred during 1975–1980, when they came out of the deep recession of 1974–1975 and undertook to build up assets in anticipation of a potential growth of demand.

In table 2.2, we have shown the compound annual growth rate of assets in five-year time intervals. Here, also, the highest or the second-highest annual growth for most firms took place during 1975–1980, in the aftermath of the economic recession of 1974–1975. For the excellent firms, this was true for those in the general industrial, project management, and resource-based groupings, whereas for firms in the high technology grouping, the more recent years (1980–1984) were the best years, during which

**Table 2.1**
**Index of Assets of the Excellent and Control Firms, 1960–1984**

| Industry Groupings | Index of Assets | | | | |
|---|---|---|---|---|---|
| | 1965 | 1970 | 1975 | 1980 | 1984 |
| **A. Excellent Firms** | | | | | |
| High Tech. | 174.59 | 373.66 | 456.67 | 917.04 | 1883.74 |
| Consumer Goods | 157.11 | 316.55 | 582.53 | 1099.22 | 1425.14 |
| General Indus. | 151.08 | 204.18 | 336.91 | 587.09 | 777.52 |
| Service | 162.43 | 384.04 | 758.82 | 1654.11 | 2781.92 |
| Project Manage. | 157.06 | 497.76 | 401.62 | 1317.91 | 2136.17 |
| Resource-Based | 131.75 | 205.80 | 360.33 | 661.63 | 847.84 |
| Total | 148.07 | 256.97 | 402.83 | 765.62 | 1154.57 |
| **B. Control Firms** | | | | | |
| High Tech. | 173.32 | 425.08 | 628.89 | 1026.12 | 1297.67 |
| Consumer Goods | 161.02 | 314.31 | 503.20 | 947.54 | 1131.76 |
| General Indus. | 178.24 | 254.89 | 365.38 | 670.64 | 807.65 |
| Service | 197.14 | 347.51 | 527.35 | 1123.77 | 1957.16 |
| Project Manage. | 98.11 | 187.61 | 235.33 | 421.56 | 519.85 |
| Resource-Based | 163.52 | 256.75 | 457.70 | 883.07 | 1294.53 |
| Total | 171.70 | 306.81 | 478.66 | 891.48 | 1234.04 |

Source: Basic data were collected from Moody's Industrial Manuals, and Moody's Transportation Manuals, various issues covering 1960-1984.

they grew, on average, at the compound annual growth rate of about 20 percent. For firms in the consumer goods sector, 1965–1970 was the period during which they registered the highest growth rate per year. Taking the entire twenty-five years into account, the highest compound annual growth rate of assets was attained by firms in the service industry, with firms in high technology coming very close behind. The least growth was attained by firms in the general industrial group, followed by firms in the resource-based group. Both showed a per annum growth rate of less than 10 percent. As an aggregate, the excellent firms grew by 10.73 percent per year during the entire period of 1960–1984.

**Table 2.2**
**Compound Annual Growth Rates of Assets of the Excellent and Control Firms, 1960–1984**

| Industry Groupings | Years | | | | | |
|---|---|---|---|---|---|---|
| | 1960-1965 | 1965-1970 | 1970-1975 | 1975-80 | 1980-84 | 1960-84 |
| A.  Excellent  Firms | | | | | | |
| High Tech. | 11.79 | 16.43 | 4.09 | 14.96 | 19.72 | 13.01 |
| Consumer Goods | 9.46 | 15.04 | 12.97 | 13.54 | 6.71 | 11.71 |
| General Indus. | 8.60 | 6.21 | 10.53 | 11.75 | 7.28 | 8.92 |
| Service | 10.19 | 18.78 | 14.59 | 16.86 | 13.88 | 14.86 |
| Project Manage. | 9.45 | 25.95 | -0.04 | 26.83 | 12.83 | 13.61 |
| Resource-Based | 5.67 | 9.33 | 11.85 | 12.92 | 6.40 | 9.31 |
| Total Assets | 8.17 | 11.66 | 9.41 | 13.70 | 10.81 | 10.73 |
| B.  Control  Firms | | | | | | |
| High Tech. | 11.63 | 19.65 | 8.15 | 10.29 | 4.81 | 11.27 |
| Consumer Goods | 9.99 | 14.31 | 9.87 | 13.49 | 4.54 | 10.63 |
| General Indus. | 12.25 | 7.42 | 7.47 | 12.91 | 4.76 | 9.09 |
| Service | 14.54 | 12.01 | 8.70 | 16.34 | 14.88 | 13.19 |
| Project Manage. | -0.38 | 13.84 | 4.64 | 12.37 | 5.38 | 7.11 |
| Resource-Based | 10.33 | 9.44 | 12.26 | 14.05 | 10.03 | 11.26 |
| TOTAL Assets | 11.42 | 12.31 | 9.30 | 13.24 | 8.47 | 11.04 |

Source: Basic data were collected from Moody's Industrial Manuals, and Moody's Transportation Manuals, various issues covering 1960-1984.

When we compare the impressive growth rate of the excellent firms with that of the control firms, however, we find that as an aggregate, the latter group did better than the former group, since the control firms grew by 11.04 percent during the same twenty-five-year period. Here, also, the highest growth rates for most of the groupings took place during 1975–1980, when the annual growth rate was highest for firms in four groupings except those in high technology and consumer goods which grew fastest during 1965–1970. That was also the period when high technology had the highest annual growth rate among all six groupings, followed by the firms in the service industry during 1975–1980. Taking the entire two and a half decades

**Table 2.3**
**Index of Sales of the Excellent and Control Firms, 1960–1984**

| Industry Groupings | Index of Sales | | | | |
|---|---|---|---|---|---|
| | 1965 | 1970 | 1975 | 1980 | 1984 |
| A. Excellent Firms | | | | | |
| High Tech. | 197.14 | 404.52 | 736.26 | 1517.42 | 2220.55 |
| Consumer Goods | 156.59 | 277.50 | 535.43 | 1031.41 | 1216.94 |
| General Indus. | 164.15 | 165.53 | 323.05 | 553.26 | 725.22 |
| Service | 183.20 | 186.82 | 1230.86 | 2367.49 | 3833.72 |
| Project Manage. | 138.42 | 250.15 | 299.13 | 845.21 | 875.04 |
| Resource-Based | 145.81 | 214.88 | 531.37 | 1269.04 | 1352.12 |
| Total | 161.83 | 240.83 | 500.13 | 1045.66 | 1298.41 |
| B. Control Firms | | | | | |
| High Tech. | 190.93 | 391.05 | 744.50 | 1073.33 | 1217.39 |
| Consumer Goods | 139.71 | 260.51 | 461.42 | 844.74 | 1033.14 |
| General Indus. | 201.36 | 279.18 | 478.77 | 838.65 | 1078.23 |
| Service | 156.73 | 250.78 | 408.81 | 714.99 | 982.52 |
| Project Manage. | 108.20 | 143.82 | 177.11 | 323.35 | 481.69 |
| Resource-Based | 165.26 | 258.43 | 760.75 | 1929.46 | 1819.48 |
| Total | 167.79 | 280.30 | 545.25 | 1027.29 | 1181.39 |

Source: Basic data were collected from Moody's Industrial Manuals,
and Moody's Transportation Manuals, various issues covering
1960-1984.

into account, the highest annual growth rate was registered by the firms in the service sector for both the excellent and the control groups.

Table 2.3 shows the index of sales for both the excellent and control firms during 1960–1984. As an aggregate, the excellent firms did somewhat better than the control firms. For the former group, the highest growth in the index of sales occurred for firms in the service sector, as was the case in the index of assets. The second-highest growth was registered by firms in the high technology industry. Resource-based firms were third in ranking. As was the case with respect to assets (table 2.1), the sales figures for firms in the general industrial group and those in project management were less impressive. Here, also, the index indicates the greatest growth during 1975–1980, except for the service sector, which had the highest growth during 1980–1984. During the period 1980–1984, however, firms in the resource-based grouping grew very sluggishly, and firms in the project management group hardly grew at all or actually lost ground.

When we look at the index of sales for the control firms, we find that through 1980 the highest growth occurred for firms in the resource-based grouping. But in 1984 this index tumbled from the previous period, although it remained highest among all the groupings for the year. For 1984, the second highest position for both excellent and control firms was occupied by firms in the high technology industry group. Firms in the service sector grew rather moderately in terms of the index of sales, and the least growth took place among firms in project management. Among control firms, except for the high technology firms, the highest rate of growth according to this index occurred during 1975–1980, followed by the 1980–1984 time period. For the high technology firms, however, the highest growth of sales took place during the recessionary period of 1970–1975. The aggregate index of sales for both the excellent and control firms rose most dramatically from 1975 to 1980, which was also true in the case of the asset index, as seen in table 2.1.

Table 2.4 presents the compound annual growth rate of sales in selected time intervals. This table shows that, on average, the excellent firms had a slightly higher growth rate than the control firms. For the excellent group, the highest annual growth rate occurred for firms in the service sector and resource-based industry group during 1970–1975, whereas the highest growth rate for firms in project management and firms in high technology took place during 1975–1980. This was also true for the firms taken as an aggregate, although they grew at almost the same rate during 1970–1975. Taking the entire twenty-five years into account, firms in the service sector had the highest average annual growth rate, followed by firms in high technology.

For the compound annual growth rates of the control firms, the resource-based industry saw the highest growth rate during the periods 1970–1975 and 1975–1980. Firms in the high technology industry grew most during 1965–1970, as was true for firms in the consumer goods industry. For the other three groupings, however, the highest annual growth rate took place during 1975–1980. As an aggregate, the highest annual growth rate of sales occurred during 1970–1975, but the rate was also quite high during 1975–1980. Encompassing the entire twenty-five-year

**Table 2.4**
**Compound Annual Growth Rates of Sales of the Excellent and Control Firms, 1960–1984**

| Industrial Groupings | Years | | | | | |
|---|---|---|---|---|---|---|
| | 1960-65 | 1965-70 | 1970-75 | 1975-80 | 1980-84 | 1960-84 |
| | | A.   Excellent   Firms | | | | |
| High Tech. | 14.54 | 15.46 | 12.72 | 15.56 | 9.99 | 13.79 |
| Consumer Goods | 9.38 | 12.12 | 14.05 | 14.01 | 4.22 | 10.97 |
| General Indus. | 10.42 | 0.17 | 14.31 | 11.36 | 7.00 | 8.61 |
| Service | 12.87 | 18.62 | 23.39 | 13.98 | 12.81 | 16.41 |
| Project Manage. | 6.72 | 12.56 | 3.64 | 23.09 | 0.87 | 9.46 |
| Resource-Based | 7.83 | 8.06 | 19.85 | 19.02 | 1.60 | 11.46 |
| Total | 10.11 | 8.28 | 15.74 | 15.89 | 5.56 | 11.27 |
| | | B.   Control   Firms | | | | |
| High Tech. | 13.81 | 15.42 | 13.42 | 13.74 | 7.59 | 10.98 |
| Consumer Goods | 6.92 | 13.27 | 12.11 | 12.86 | 5.16 | 10.22 |
| General Indus. | 15.03 | 6.75 | 11.39 | 11.86 | 6.48 | 10.41 |
| Service | 9.40 | 9.86 | 10.27 | 11.83 | 8.27 | 9.99 |
| Project Manage. | 1.59 | 5.86 | 4.25 | 12.79 | 10.48 | 6.77 |
| Resource-Based | 10.57 | 9.35 | 24.10 | 20.46 | -1.46 | 12.85 |
| Total | 10.91 | 10.81 | 14.23 | 13.51 | 3.56 | 10.84 |

Source: Basic data were collected from Moody's Industrial Manuals,
and Moody's Transportation Manuals, various issues covering
1960-1984.

period, the highest annual growth rate of sales took place for firms in resource-based industry, although their annual growth rate was negative during 1980–1984. Firms in high technology had the second-highest annual growth rate, which was also true for this sector in the excellent firms sample, as seen in table 2.2.

Both table 2.2 and table 2.4 show that the positions of most firms deteriorated during 1980–1984, as compared to 1975–1980, and that the annual growth rates of both assets and sales slowed down considerably during the latest period of the study. Michelle Clayman also found this to be the case in her study of these excellent firms when she compared the situation in 1981–1985 with that of 1976–1980.[3] The slower annual growth of assets and sales was more pronounced for the excellent firms than the control firms, as can be seen by comparing both tables. In the excellent firms sample, the annual growth rate of assets had been reduced by almost half or more in three out of the six groupings in 1980–1984 as compared to 1975–1980, while the annual growth rate of sales delined precipitously in four out of the six groupings. This was also true for the control firms in most of the groupings. However, this parity in decline is particularly ironic for the excellent firms which, after all, should show above-average growth rates to warrant their excellent rating.

In table 2.5, we give a summary statistic of the size distribution of firms classified by the annual growth rate of assets. During the 1960–1984 period, 37 percent of the firms in the control group had, on average, a growth rate of less than 15 percent per year, while for the excellent group, the percentage of firms belonging to this class was above 60 percent. The control group, however, also had two firms in the highest annual growth class (i.e., 25 percent above), while in the excellent group there were none in this category. By the criterion of growth rate of assets alone, these companies of the control group (such as Occidental Petroleum) should have been a part of the excellent group, while companies such as Caterpillar Tractor or Fluor Corporation should have been dropped from the list long ago.

## GROWTH OF EARNINGS OF THE EXCELLENT AND CONTROL FIRMS, 1960–1984

Corporate earning is another important measure of financial performance. Growth of earnings and the quality of earnings growth are reflections of a firm's performance to itself and to its stockholders. They indicate its ability to finance internally any future expansion of its facilities and businesses.[4] Expected earnings and profitability depend very much on past earnings and the percentage of these earnings that derive from sales. This is particularly important for the excellent firm, which should demonstrate an above-average growth of earnings and price per share. Above all, they should be excellent to investors who are looking for strong and stable growth of earnings on a long-term basis.

In this section, we have estimated the net profit margins of both the excellent and control firms, as well as the growth of earnings per share of these firms. Net profit margin is calculated by dividing net sales or revenues into net earnings. The earnings per share is estimated by dividing the number of shares outstanding into net earnings. Since firms do resort to stock splits and stock dividends occasionally, these steps will dilute the

**Table 2.5**
**Number and Percentage Distribution of the Excellent and Control Firms by the Growth Rates of Assets, 1960–1984**

| Annual Growth Rates of Assets | Excellent Firms (1960-1984) | | Control Firms (1960-1984) | |
|---|---|---|---|---|
| | No. | % | No. | % |
| Below 10% | 10 | 21.28 | 19 | 37.26 |
| 10% - 15% | 18 | 38.30 | 25 | 49.02 |
| 15% - 20% | 13 | 27.66 | 3 | 5.88 |
| 20% - 25% | 6 | 12.76 | 2 | 3.92 |
| 25% & Above | -- | --- | 2 | 3.92 |
| Total | 47 | 100.00 | 51 | 100.00 |

Source: Basic data were collected from Moody's Industrial Manuals and Moody's Transportation Manuals, various issues covering 1960-1984.

number of shares outstanding, which, in turn, will affect the calculation of the earnings per share. In order to obtain the "true" earnings per share, we have to estimate the adjusted earnings per share over time. This we have done for our samples of both the excellent and the control firms.

In table 2.6, we show the average net profit margins of the excellent and the control firms for the selected years, covering 1960–1984. For the excellent firms, the mean return on sales was highest for the firms in the consumer goods industry, followed by firms in the resource-based industry. Here the firms in high technology stood fourth, and firms in the service sector were fifth. The last place was occupied by the firms in project management, which earned a mean rate of 3.01 percent. As an aggregate, the mean profit margin of the excellent firms for the entire twenty-five-year period was 6.01 percent.

For the control firms, the highest mean return on sales was earned by the resource-based firms, followed by firms in the consumer goods industry. Here, also, the high technology firms took fourth place, but last place was occupied by the service whose profit margin in sales is generally low throughout the economy. As a group, the mean profit margin of the control firms for the 1960–1984 period was 4.77 percent, thus indicating that the excellent firms did somewhat better on this score during the period covered by our study.

**Table 2.6**

**Average Net Profit Margins of the Excellent and Control Firms, 1960–1984**

| Industry Groupings | Years | | | | | |
|---|---|---|---|---|---|---|
| | 1960 | 1965 | 1970 | 1975 | 1980 | 1984 |
| A. Excellent Firms | | | | | | |
| High Tech. | 4.48 | 6.92 | 3.30 | 6.33 | 6.97 | 6.99 |
| Consumer Goods | 8.08 | 10.24 | 9.22 | 8.28 | 8.33 | 6.39 |
| General Indus. | 8.80 | 10.22 | 7.26 | 7.24 | 4.81 | 2.07 |
| Service | 1.48 | 6.99 | 5.45 | 4.10 | 5.26 | 5.21 |
| Project Manage. | 1.80 | 3.40 | 1.75 | 2.75 | 4.55 | 3.81 |
| Resource-Based | 10.36 | 9.66 | 7.58 | 6.94 | 6.52 | 5.56 |
| Total | 5.83 | 7.91 | 5.76 | 5.94 | 6.07 | 5.01 |
| B. Control Firms | | | | | | |
| High Tech. | 3.96 | 5.43 | 3.81 | 3.14 | 4.36 | 4.07 |
| Consumer Goods | 5.45 | 6.87 | 6.30 | 5.50 | 5.82 | 6.82 |
| General Indus. | 7.66 | 7.01 | 4.39 | 3.34 | 6.41 | 3.83 |
| Service | 3.00 | 4.36 | 1.36 | 1.31 | 2.24 | 3.28 |
| Project Manage. | 3.12 | 3.76 | 4.67 | 4.12 | 4.47 | 3.92 |
| Resource-Based | 8.36 | 8.60 | 6.40 | 4.90 | 4.86 | 4.76 |
| Total | 5.62 | 6.01 | 4.49 | 3.72 | 4.69 | 4.45 |

Source: Basic data were collected from Moody's Industrial Manuals
        and Moody's Transportation Manuals, various issues covering
        1960-1984.

When we examine the percentage change in net profit margins in selected time intervals, as shown in table 2.7, we find that for the excellent firms, 1965–1970 was the worst period. Net profit margins declined for all six industry groupings, with the worst decline occurring in firms in the high technology industry. For the latter grouping, the highest growth occurred during 1970–1975, when the profit margins almost doubled from the previous time interval. The years 1960–1965 were the best period in profit margins for four out of the six industry groupings, namely, consumer goods, general industrial, service, and project management. For the resource-based firms, however, profit margins declined from the very beginning of the period. Over the entire period of 1960–1984, the percentage

**Tables 2.7**
**Percentage Change in Net Profit Margins of the Excellent and Control Firms in Selected Time Intervals**

| Industry Groupings | Years | | | | | |
|---|---|---|---|---|---|---|
| | 1960–1965 | 1965–1970 | 1970–1975 | 1975–1980 | 1980–1984 | 1960–1984 |
| A. Excellent Firms | | | | | | |
| High Tech. | 54.56 | -52.31 | 91.82 | 10.11 | 0.29 | 56.03 |
| Consumer Goods | 26.73 | -9.96 | -10.19 | 0.60 | -23.28 | -20.92 |
| General Indus. | 16.14 | -28.96 | -0.28 | -33.56 | -56.96 | -76.47 |
| Service | 372.30 | -22.03 | -24.77 | 28.29 | -0.95 | 252.03 |
| Project Manage. | 88.89 | -48.53 | 57.14 | 65.45 | -16.26 | 111.67 |
| Resource-Based | -6.76 | -21.53 | -8.44 | -6.05 | -14.72 | -46.33 |
| B. Control Firms | | | | | | |
| High Tech. | 37.12 | -29.83 | -17.59 | 38.85 | -6.65 | 2.77 |
| Consumer Goods | 20.06 | -8.30 | -12.70 | 5.82 | 17.18 | 25.14 |
| General Indus. | -8.49 | -37.38 | -23.92 | 91.92 | -47.27 | -50.00 |
| Service | 45.53 | -68.80 | -3.68 | 68.38 | 46.43 | 9.33 |
| Project Manage. | 20.51 | 24.20 | -11.77 | 8.50 | -12.30 | 25.64 |
| Resource-Based | 2.87 | -25.58 | -23.44 | -0.82 | -2.06 | -43.06 |

Source: Basic data were collected from Moody's Industrial Manuals and Moody's Transportation Manuals, various issues covering 1960-1984.

increase of the profit margin was the highest for the firms in the service sector, but they were negative for firms in the consumer goods, general industrial, and resource-based industries. As a group, the percentage change in net profit margins was −14.07 percent during 1960–1984.

For the percentage change of net profit margins of the control firms, the worst period occurred in 1970–1975, as they fell off in all six groupings. Comparatively, the best period was during 1975–1980, when five groupings had positive growth rates in profit margins. The exception to this trend was the resource-based firms, which dipped slightly. As an aggregate, the percentage change in net profit margins was −15.40 percent during 1960–1984. It is important to note, however, that for both the excellent and control firms the net profit margins had deteriorated during 1980–1984, as compared to 1975–1980. The decline was more severe, however, for the excellent firms, whose profit margins fell in five out of six industry groupings and remained the same in one, while for the control firms they fell in four out of six groupings and increased considerably in the other two industry groupings. Nowhere do we witness any long-term stable or positive growth rates of the net profit margins, about which investors would be concerned.

In table 2.8, we show the adjusted average earnings per share of those 86 industrial companies listed in *Fortune* magazine's largest 500 U.S. industrial corporations in 1985, which were divided equally in our samples of the excellent and control firms.[5] The earnings per share were adjusted to take account of stock splits or significant stock dividend actions in these companies during the time period 1974–1984. (Since we are concerned only with manufacturing companies in our two samples, the service sector has been omitted in this table.) Here we find that for the excellent firms, the highest annual compound growth rate in earnings per share was obtained by firms in project management. However, there were only two firms in this grouping, and there is a statistical bias inherent in such a very small sample. The second-highest growth rate occurred for firms in the high technology industry, followed by firms in the consumer goods industry. Both for resource-based firms as well as for firms in general industrial, the growth of earnings per share was quite modest during 1974–1984.

When we look into the growth of the earnings per share of the control firms in this period, we find that the highest growth rate was obtained by the firms in the consumer goods industry group, following by firms in the high technology group. The comparative growth of firms in general industrial and project management was virtually the same. The least growth was obtained by firms in the resource-based industry, which witnessed some rough times and changes of fortune during this decade. This table shows that the average earnings per share for the excellent firms as a group were much higher than for firms in the control group during this period. However, if we exclude the two project management firms because of biases inherent in very small samples, we find that the mean annual growth rate of earnings per share was slightly higher (6.85%) for the control group than for the excellent group (6.16%) for the period 1974–1984.

As a matter of fact, when we rank the thirty leading firms of both the excellent and control groups according to the ten-year average rate of

**Table 2.8**
**Adjusted Average Earnings per Share of the Excellent and Control Industrial Companies, 1974–1984**

| Industry Groupings | Years | | |
|---|---|---|---|
| | 1974 | 1984 | Compound Annual Growth Rates (%) |
| **A. Excellent Firms** | | | |
| High Tech. | $1.50 | $4.36 | 11.26 |
| Consumer Goods | 1.79 | 3.76 | 7.70 |
| General Indus. | 3.12 | 4.42 | 3.54 |
| Project Manage. | 0.76 | 8.09 | 26.68 |
| Resource-Based | 2.95 | 5.13 | 5.69 |
| **B. Control Firms** | | | |
| High Tech. | $1.60 | $3.14 | 6.97 |
| Consumer Goods | 1.24 | 4.41 | 13.53 |
| General Indus. | 2.09 | 3.59 | 5.56 |
| Project Manage. | 2.19 | 3.62 | 5.15 |
| Resource-Based | 3.69 | 4.22 | 1.35 |

Source: Basic data were collected from _Fortune_, April 29,1985, Pp. 266-285.

earnings per share, as shown in table 2.9, we find the number of ranks in both these groups are in a tie (i.e., fifteen each), thus indicating no overall superiority by the excellent firms in this regard. Although Westinghouse and Boeing had the number 2 and number 4 positions, respectively, the number 1 spot was occupied by Wang Laboratories, a much smaller company in the excellent group. Similarly, in the control group, the highest ranking was obtained by Control Data, followed by Johnson Controls (number 3 and number 5, respectively), which were also much smaller in size among this group. This shows again the folly of selecting mainly the largest firms in Peters and Waterman's list of excellent firms. When we try to analyze the various financial situations of these companies, we notice that big is not necessarily better, and that the relatively smaller

**Table 2.9**
**Ranking of Industrial Firms by 10-Year EPS Growth (1974–1984)**

| Name of the Firm | Ranking by ESP Growth (10-Year) |
|---|:---:|
| Wang Laboratories (E) | 1 |
| Westinghouse Electric (E) | 2 |
| Control Data (C) | 3 |
| Boeing Co. (E) | 4 |
| Johnson Controls (C) | 5 |
| Lockheed (E) | 6 |
| Ford Motor Co. (C) | 7 |
| Hewlett-Packard (E) | 8 |
| Northrop Corp. (C) | 9 |
| Intel Corp. (E) | 10 |
| | |
| Data General (E) | 11 |
| Philip Morris (C) | 12 |
| Digital Equipment (E) | 13 |
| General Motors (E) | 14 |
| Zenith Corp. (C) | 15 |
| Motorola (C) | 16 |
| Cabot Corp. (C) | 17 |
| IBM (E) | 18 |
| Borg-Warner (C) | 19 |
| Kellogg Corp. (C) | 20 |
| | |
| Texas Instruments (E) | 21 |
| Raychem (E) | 22 |
| Pfizer (C) | 23 |
| Rockwell (E) | 24 |
| General Mills (C) | 25 |
| American Home Products (C) | 26 |
| Pillsbury (C) | 27 |
| Emerson Electric (E) | 28 |
| General Electric (E) | 29 |
| Raytheon (C) | 30 |

(E) - Excellent Firms.
(C) - Control Firms.

Source: Fortune, April 29, 1985, pp. 266-85

firms can outshine the giant and dominating firms in terms of many important aspects of financial performance.

## RETURNS TO STOCKHOLDERS BY THE EXCELLENT AND CONTROL FIRMS, 1960–1984

Since stockholders are the true owners of public corporations, the return they receive for owning shares of these companies should be the prime consideration in evaluating their financial performance. If the management's primary goal is to maximize the wealth of its stockholders, then the returns of the latter group from these stocks, which include price appreciation of the shares over time, should be the main concern of the management. And if the managers of the large firms seem to make decisions that are largely oriented toward stock price maximization, as Lewellen had found, then the stockholders of these essentially large excellent firms should be obtaining not only the above-average returns, but benefitting from the sustained growth of these returns over a long period of time.[6] Since the returns achieved by a corporation or its investors are the results of risks undertaken, we are mainly concerned with the risk-adjusted returns, that is, stock or portfolio returns that are commensurate with the risks involved, however they are measured.

In table 2.10, we have estimated the returns on investment (ROI) of the excellent and control firms during 1960–1984, by dividing net earnings by the total assets of the firm. For the excellent group, the highest mean return on investment was received by firms in the consumer goods industry, followed by the revenue-based industry. The lowest mean return was shown by the service industry, which is characterized by low profit margins in the economy as a whole. We also find that the return was uneven for every industry throughout the entire period. It was highest in the consumer goods industry in 1965, but then declined in almost all selected years. The sharpest decline took place during 1965–1970, when the return on investment fell for all six groupings. As an aggregate, the mean return on investment was 7.78 percent for the twenty-five-year period.

When we examine the return on investment for the control group, we find that the pattern is strikingly similar; the mean return was also highest for the firms in the consumer goods industry, followed by the resource-based industry. Here, also, the lowest mean return was received by firms in the service industry. Moreover, the returns were uneven throughout the selected periods, and all the ROI's in six groupings fell in 1970, which was one of the best years in the post–World War II period in terms of economic prosperity, as compared to 1965. As a group, the mean return on investment for the control firms was 6.65 percent, over 1 percentage point lower than the excellent group over the entire period. But we also notice the fact—found in many other earlier calculations—that the returns on investment in most of the groups deteriorated from 1980 to 1984. This deterioration was most evident for the excellent firms, where the ROI's fell in five out of the six groupings (staying virtually the same in the remaining grouping). In contrast, among the control firms, they fell in only three of the six groupings during the latest period of our study.

**Table 2.10**
**Return on Investment of the Excellent and Control Firms, 1960–1984**

| Industry Groupings | Years | | | | | |
|---|---|---|---|---|---|---|
| | 1960 | 1965 | 1970 | 1975 | 1980 | 1984 |
| A. Excellent Firms | | | | | | |
| High Tech. | 6.12 | 9.23 | 4.21 | 7.39 | 8.28 | 7.77 |
| Consumer Goods | 12.22 | 15.39 | 12.28 | 11.46 | 11.48 | 8.24 |
| General Ind. | 10.83 | 13.83 | 8.34 | 8.50 | 5.50 | 3.83 |
| Service | 2.28 | 8.55 | 5.08 | 5.03 | 6.07 | 6.49 |
| Project Manage. | 5.35 | 8.15 | 3.25 | 6.45 | 8.90 | 4.66 |
| Resource-Based | 8.10 | 8.18 | 6.22 | 7.02 | 8.78 | 6.60 |
| Total | 7.48 | 10.56 | 6.56 | 7.64 | 8.17 | 6.26 |
| B. Control Firms | | | | | | |
| High Tech. | 6.04 | 7.42 | 5.79 | 3.91 | 6.31 | 5.75 |
| Consumer Goods | 8.52 | 9.72 | 8.07 | 9.62 | 8.98 | 9.26 |
| General Ind. | 8.92 | 6.35 | 4.34 | 4.59 | 7.49 | 3.81 |
| Service | 6.53 | 7.41 | 3.91 | 3.01 | 3.95 | 5.36 |
| Project Manage. | 6.85 | 7.65 | 4.80 | 4.70 | 6.25 | 7.70 |
| Resource-Based | 6.89 | 7.37 | 5.40 | 7.68 | 11.76 | 7.38 |
| Total | 7.29 | 7.65 | 5.38 | 5.60 | 7.46 | 6.54 |

Source: Basic data were collected from Moody's Industrial Manuals
        and Moody's Transportation Manuals, various issues covering
        1960-1984.

We have also calculated the risk-adjusted returns of the excellent and control firms, making them into two respective portfolios. According to the Capital Asset Pricing Model (CAPM), there are two types of portfolio risks—unsystematic (alpha or firm-specific) risk and the systematic (beta or market) risk. Whereas the unsystematic risk can be eliminated by judicious diversifications of the portfolio, particularly following the rules of Professor Harry Markowitz, systematic risk has to be taken into account to determine the risk-adjusted return.[7] Thus the value of beta tells us about the risk of the stock relative to the market, that is, a beta higher than 1 means the stock is riskier than the market, and vice versa, while a beta value of 1 indicates the stock is as risky as the market itself.

In order to measure the risk-adjusted returns of the portfolio,[8] we may calculate Sharpe's reward-to-variability ratio, $[R - Rf]/[S(R)]$, where, for specific period: $R$ = stockholder return comprised of capital gains and dividends; $Rf$ = risk-free return (90-day T-bill rate); and $S(R)$ = standard deviation for the periodic returns during the investment horizon.

Sharpe's measure provides ordinal ranking of return per unit of total risk. This is particularly important to investors with limited diversification. However, investors who are well-diversified are interested in a stock's contribution to the systematic risk. For that, we have to calculate Treynor's measure as follows:

$[R - Rf]/B$, where

$B$ = estimated beta of the stock determined by the market model

$[R - Rf] = a + B[Rm - Rf] + e$ where, for a specified period

$a$ = intercept term (alpha or abnormal return)

$Rm$ = return on the market (index); and

$e$ = error term of the regression equation.

The third risk-adjusted measure that we employ, Jensen's alpha, is related to the Treynor measure. It is the intercept term of the market model defined above. If investors' expectations with regard to systematic risk and return are fulfilled, then alpha should be zero. However, if performance is either superior or inferior to the model's prediction, then alpha will be positive or negative, respectively.

Peters and Waterman divided their sample into three categories: Top Performers, Exemplar, and (ordinary) Excellent. Top Performers were those twenty-two firms that ranked in the top half of their respective industry in at least four of the six financial performance measures for the entire period 1961–1980, and also were rated by the industry experts as "continuously innovative." The fourteen Exemplar firms not only passed the screening for Top Performers, but also were rated by Peters and Waterman as embodying the eight attributes of excellent management. In our tests we compare the performance of the three subgroups with each other; we compare their performance with the performance of the total excellent sample, and with our control portfolio, which is composed of a slightly different and smaller sample (consisting of thirty-two firms) than the full sample listed in table 1.5. For the market index, we have used the equally weighted index of all NYSE stocks as contained in the CRSP tapes.

In table 2.11, we show the returns of the two risk-adjusted portfolios as well as the performance of the market index. Columns (1), (4), and (7) present the number of years during three subperiods of the 1960–1984 period that the excellent firm portfolios outperformed the market index. Columns (2), (5), and (8) present the number of years that the excellent firms' portfolios outperformed the control portfolio in these periods. The subperiods were 1960–1969, 1970–1979, and 1980–1984. Here we evaluate performance using mean returns, the Treynor measure, and the Sharpe measure. The average monthly portfolio values of these performance measures during the three subperiods are reported in columns (3), (6), and (9).

The data in table 2.11 also confirm our earlier findings of a deterioration in the relative performance of excellent firms over time. For example, for the ten-year period 1960–1969, we find that the excellent portfolios outperformed the market index and the control portfolio for five or more years, with few exceptions. (The performance of ordinary excellent firms measured by mean returns and the Sharpe measure shows only four years in which they outperformed the market.) In the 1970–1979 period, relatively few measures indicate that the market or control firms were outperformed by the excellent firms. (Only the Exemplar subsample outperformed the control firms, according to the Sharpe and Treynor measures, for more than five of the ten years.) The average monthly returns reported for both periods tend to confirm these yearly findings.

The 1980–1984 results suggest continuing deterioration of shareholder returns among the excellent firms, thus validating the poorer financial performance reported for that period by Clayman. The excellent firms outperformed the market for two or less years according to all measures, although they generally outperformed the control firms in three of the five years. Again, these results are supported by the average monthly returns of the period.

Table 2.12 presents further evidence of degenerating investment performance of the excellent firms. Portfolio average monthly alphas of the Jensen measure are presented for each five-year subperiod for each subsample. All but one alpha was positive for the first three subperiods, indicating superior performance. In contrast, for the last two subperiods all but one excellent subsample have negative alphas, indicating inferior performance. Obviously, the shareholders of the excellent firms did not earn any markedly superior returns as compared to the control firms, or the average returns of the market, particularly during the last five years of our study.

Table 2.11

**Portfolio Comparisons—Number of Years Excellent Portfolios Outperformed Market and Control Portfolios for Three Subperiods**

| Measures and Portfolios | 1960-1969 Excellent vs. MKT | CTRL | 10-Year Mean Values | 1970-1979 Excellent vs. MKT | CTRL | 10-Year Mean Values | 1980-1984 Excellent vs. MKT | CTRL | 5-Year Mean Values |
|---|---|---|---|---|---|---|---|---|---|
| Column Nos. | (1) | (2) | (3) | (4) | (5) | (6) | (7) | (8) | (9) |
| Mean Returns |  |  |  |  |  |  |  |  |  |
| Excellent | 7 | 8 | .0100 | 4 | 4 | .0051 | 1 | 3 | .0105 |
| Ordinary Exc. | 4 | 5 | .0066 | 3 | 4 | .0043 | 0 | 3 | .0118 |
| Top Performers | 5 | 7 | .0108 | 4 | 4 | .0046 | 2 | 3 | .0100 |
| Exemplar | 8 | 8 | .0143 | 4 | 5 | .0073 | 2 | 2 | .0096 |
| Control |  |  | .0084 |  |  | .0066 |  |  | .0109 |
| Market |  |  | .0089 |  |  | .0080 |  |  | .0478 |
| Sharpe |  |  |  |  |  |  |  |  |  |
| Excellent | 8 | 9 | .1537 | 5 | 4 | -.0021 | 1 | 3 | .0285 |
| Ordinary Exc. | 4 | 6 | .0755 | 3 | 3 | -.0161 | 2 | 3 | .0504 |
| Top Performers | 6 | 7 | .1670 | 4 | 4 | -.0103 | 0 | 3 | .0181 |
| Exemplar | 7 | 8 | .2154 | 5 | 6 | -.0341 | 2 | 3 | .0097 |
| Control |  |  | .1060 |  |  | -.0026 |  |  | .0182 |
| Market |  |  | .1266 |  |  | .0429 |  |  | .1146 |
| Treynor |  |  |  |  |  |  |  |  |  |
| Excellent | 8 | 9 | .0074 | 3 | 4 | -.0002 | 1 | 3 | .0016 |
| Ordinary Exc. | 5 | 6 | .0038 | 3 | 3 | -.0012 | 2 | 3 | .0028 |
| Top Performers | 7 | 7 | .0083 | 3 | 4 | -.0009 | 2 | 3 | .0010 |
| Exemplar | 8 | 8 | .0110 | 4 | 6 | .0027 | 1 | 2 | .0006 |
| Control |  |  | .0050 |  |  | .0050 |  |  | .0018 |
| Market |  |  | .0056 |  |  | .0027 |  |  | .0057 |

N.B.  All measures are based on monthly returns.

Source: Kolodny, R., M. Laurence, and Arabinda Ghosh, "In Search of Excellence...For Whom?" (Working Paper, 1988)

**Table 2.12**
**Portfolio Alphas**

| Portfolios | 1960-1964 | 1965-1969 | 1970-1974 | 1975-1979 | 1980-1984 |
|---|---|---|---|---|---|
| Excellent (total) | .0051 | .0041 | .0052 | -.0015 | -.0012 |
| Ordinary Excellent | .0055 | -.0012 | .0013 | -.0012 | .0000 |
| Top Performers | .0019 | .0071 | .0051 | -.0024 | -.0014 |
| Exemplar | .0090 | .0074 | .0108 | -.0006 | -.0026 |
| Control | .0008 | .0029 | .0027 | .0028 | -.0012 |
| Market | 0 | 0 | 0 | 0 | 0 |

Source: Kolodny, R., M. Laurence, and Arabinda Ghosh, "In
Search of Excellence...For Whom?" (Working Paper, 1988)

## NOTES

1. Willliam Sharpe, "Mutual Fund Performance," *Journal of Business*, Vol. 39 (Jan. 1966): 119-38; Jack Treynor, "How to Rate Management of Investment Funds," *Harvard Business Review*, Vol. 43 (Jan.-Feb. 1965): 63-75; Michael Jensen, "The Performance of Mutual Funds in the Period 1945-1964," *Journal of Finance*, Vol. 23 (May 1968): 389-416.

2. Victor Fuchs, "Economic Growth and the Rise of Service Employment," in *Towards an Explanation of Economic Growth*, ed. Herbert Giersch (Tubingen, W. Germany: J. C. B. Mohr, 1981), pp. 221-22.

3. Michelle Clayman, "In Search of Excellence—The Investor's Viewpoint," *Financial Analysts' Journal*, Vol. 43 (May-June 1987): 54-63.

4. Joel Siegel, "The Quality of Earnings Concept—A Survey," *Financial Analysts' Journal*, Vol. 38 (March-April 1982): 60-64.

5. *Fortune*, April 29, 1985, pp. 266-85.

6. Wilbur Lewellen, "Management and Ownership in the Large Firm," *Journal of Finance*, Vol. 24 (May 1969): 299-322.

7. Harry Markowitz, "Portfolio Selection," *Journal of Finance*, Vol. 7 (March 1952): 77-91.

8. For a brief description of the indexes, see Frank Reilly, *Investment Analysis and Portfolio Management* (Hinsdale, Illinois: Dryden Press, 1985), pp. 677-89.

# 3

# Financial Ratios and Operating Efficiency of the United States' Excellent Firms

The analysis of the financial ratios of a firm is an important tool to measure its performance. By comparing these ratios over time, we may gauge the strengths or weaknesses of a firm in a particular area of operation or in its entirety, while the comparison of the ratios with the firm's competitors or the industry average will give us clues regarding its relative performance at a given point of time. Since the rapid decline or exceptional growth of a firm usually does not take place in a year or two, any trend analysis of the key financial ratios of a company will reveal its growing robustness or encroaching decline, leading either to its selection in the pantheon of excellent firms or to deep financial trouble in future years.[1] An important offshoot of the financial ratio analysis is its predictiveness of future bankruptcy of a firm, as the discriminant analysis developed by Robert Altman demonstrates.[2]

There are generally four types of financial ratios—liquidity ratios, leverage or debt ratios, turnover or activity ratios, and the profitability ratios. The liquidity ratios emphasize the current financial health of the company concerned (i.e., whether it would be able to pay all its bills come due, and whether its average cash position would hold for the duration of the year). The leverage ratios, on the other hand, point to the general indebtedness of a company, particularly the proportion of its long-term debt to total assets or net worth, and how many times its sales or operating income can cover the interest and other fixed charges it has to pay in a year. The turnover or activity ratios measure, among other things, the efficiency of converting the firm's inventory or other assets into sales and the receipt of cash. The profitability ratios measure the net earnings as percentage of its sales, assets, or stockholders' equity. Since we have already discussed the key profitability measures of the excellent firms in chapter 2, and will analyze the principal leverage ratios in the next chapter, it is appropriate to concentrate in this chapter only on the liquidity and turnover ratios of the excellent and control firms.

While our main objective here is to examine the financial performance of the excellent and comparative control firms in terms of various financial ratios, we should not, however, lose sight of the many limitations inherent in this type of analysis. To begin with, the shortcomings of the financial data as contained in the balance sheet and income statement of a company are too well known to warrant delineating here fully.[3] While they provide vital information about a firm, they do so only at one point in time, like a snapshot of a race, but remain silent about the intra-year performance of the firm. Then, too, there are many distortions of the financial data due to different ways of calculating depreciations by different firms, as well as the various ways of valuating inventories. Moreover, the leasing of assets instead of buying them on borrowed funds may also hide the true picture, although according to the recent directives of the Financial Accounting Standard Board (FASB), they should be disclosed in footnotes whenever necessary. Finally, a period of high inflation, such as the one we witnessed in the late 1970s, would also distort the data considerably. Although inflation affects the firms, all are not affected uniformly. Thus the examination of any financial data must be done carefully so that a true picture of the direction in which the firm is heading can be brought out clearly and within the proper context of the analysis.

## LIQUIDITY RATIOS AND CASH FLOWS OF THE EXCELLENT AND CONTROL FIRMS, 1960–1984

In tables 3.1 and 3.2, we have estimated the three types of liquidity ratios, namely, the current ratio, the acid-test ratio, and the ratio of net working capital to total assets for both the excellent and control firms in six selected periods covering 1960–1984. The current ratio is calculated by dividing the total current assets of a firm by its total current liabilities, while the acid-test or "quick" ratio is computed by dividing the firm's current assets less inventory by its current liabilities. The working capital to total assets ratio is obtained by dividing the total assets of a firm into its net working capital. It indicates the net liquidity position of a firm in relation to its total assets (i.e., the net current utilization of its assets).

**Table 3.1**
**Liquidity Ratios of the Excellent Firms for Selected Years, 1960–1984**

| Industry Groupings | Years | | | | | |
|---|---|---|---|---|---|---|
| | 1960 | 1965 | 1970 | 1975 | 1980 | 1984 |

A. Current Ratios

| | 1960 | 1965 | 1970 | 1975 | 1980 | 1984 |
|---|---|---|---|---|---|---|
| High Tech. | 2.58 | 2.13 | 2.15 | 2.33 | 2.15 | 1.93 |
| Consumer Goods | 3.08 | 2.90 | 2.95 | 2.84 | 2.50 | 2.34 |
| General Indus. | 3.07 | 2.75 | 2.43 | 2.31 | 1.98 | 1.80 |
| Service | 1.84 | 1.68 | 1.45 | 1.50 | 1.45 | 1.43 |
| Project Manage. | 1.81 | 1.74 | 1.56 | 1.54 | 1.27 | 1.27 |
| Resource-Based | 3.03 | 2.69 | 1.95 | 1.58 | 1.45 | 1.29 |

B. Acid-test Ratios

| | 1960 | 1965 | 1970 | 1975 | 1980 | 1984 |
|---|---|---|---|---|---|---|
| High Tech. | 1.60 | 1.23 | 1.30 | 1.33 | 1.25 | 1.26 |
| Consumer Goods | 1.88 | 1.80 | 1.82 | 1.64 | 1.47 | 1.83 |
| General Indus. | 1.85 | 1.53 | 1.21 | 1.15 | 1.02 | 1.03 |
| Service | 1.09 | 1.19 | 1.04 | 0.78 | 0.84 | 0.77 |
| Project Manage. | 1.36 | 1.43 | 0.83 | 0.84 | 0.85 | 0.70 |
| Resource-Based | 1.94 | 1.78 | 1.22 | 1.06 | 0.94 | 0.80 |

C. Working Capital/Total Assets

| | 1960 | 1965 | 1970 | 1975 | 1980 | 1984 |
|---|---|---|---|---|---|---|
| High Tech. | 0.34 | 0.32 | 0.30 | 0.29 | 0.28 | 0.24 |
| Consumer Goods | 0.41 | 0.42 | 0.39 | 0.41 | 0.37 | 0.26 |
| General Indus. | 0.36 | 0.39 | 0.37 | 0.32 | 0.26 | 0.22 |
| Service | 0.16 | 0.17 | 0.11 | 0.14 | 0.08 | 0.10 |
| Project Manage. | 0.31 | 0.27 | 0.21 | 0.19 | 0.13 | 0.12 |
| Resource-Based | 0.16 | 0.19 | 0.14 | 0.13 | 0.12 | 0.10 |

Source: Basic data were collected from Moody's Industrial Manuals, various issues covering 1960 - 1984.

**Table 3.2**
**Liquidity Ratios of the Control Firms for Selected Years, 1960–1984**

| Industry Groupings | Years | | | | | |
|---|---|---|---|---|---|---|
| | 1960 | 1965 | 1970 | 1975 | 1980 | 1984 |
| **A. Current Ratios** | | | | | | |
| High Tech. | 2.92 | 2.65 | 2.35 | 2.17 | 1.98 | 1.99 |
| Consumer Goods | 2.82 | 2.40 | 1.97 | 2.29 | 1.99 | 1.83 |
| General Indus. | 3.01 | 2.51 | 2.22 | 2.14 | 1.75 | 1.46 |
| Service | 2.40 | 2.19 | 1.71 | 1.66 | 1.35 | 1.48 |
| Project Manage. | 1.71 | 1.91 | 2.05 | 2.51 | 2.58 | 1.65 |
| Resource-Based | 2.90 | 2.01 | 1.86 | 1.92 | 1.30 | 1.90 |
| **B. Acid-test Ratios** | | | | | | |
| High Tech. | 1.53 | 1.42 | 1.17 | 1.08 | 0.98 | 1.11 |
| Consumer Goods | 1.38 | 1.23 | 1.12 | 1.36 | 1.08 | 1.17 |
| General Indus. | 1.67 | 1.29 | 1.07 | 0.91 | 0.89 | 0.87 |
| Service | 1.38 | 1.27 | 0.98 | 0.95 | 0.79 | 0.82 |
| Project Manage. | 0.71 | 1.31 | 1.06 | 1.07 | 1.20 | 0.98 |
| Resource-Based | 2.11 | 1.37 | 1.23 | 1.27 | 0.83 | 1.38 |
| **C. Working Capital/Total Assets** | | | | | | |
| High Tech. | 0.36 | 0.35 | 0.24 | 0.25 | 0.27 | 0.25 |
| Consumer Goods | 0.35 | 0.28 | 0.25 | 0.28 | 0.25 | 0.22 |
| General Indus. | 0.36 | 0.27 | 0.25 | 0.22 | 0.17 | 0.11 |
| Service | 0.21 | 0.19 | 0.12 | 0.14 | 0.07 | 0.16 |
| Project Manage. | 0.27 | 0.26 | 0.25 | 0.33 | 0.36 | 0.20 |
| Resource-Based | 0.21 | 0.17 | 0.17 | 0.16 | 0.11 | 0.11 |

Source: Basic data were collected from Moody's <u>Industrial Manuals</u>, various issues covering 1960-1984.

When we examine the current ratio of the excellent firms in table 3.1, we find that the ratio declined in all six industry groupings during 1960–1984. The decline was most severe in the resource-based sector, while in the service sector the decline was very modest during this twenty-five-year period. Also, in both the resource-based and the general industrial sectors the ratio declined almost uninterruptedly throughout the entire period, while in the high technology and service sectors it showed slight improvement in 1975 as compared to 1970, and then fell back again in the later periods. The current ratio for *all* the industry groupings shows the worsening situation during 1975–1984, as already indicated by other measures of the excellent firms in the later years of our study.

As for the acid-test ratio, the same trend of deterioration was evident in all six industry groupings, although for the consumer goods sector, the deterioration was quite negligible. But here, too, the decline was most severe in the resource-based sector, where it fell almost continuously by over 58 percent during 1960–1984, while for the firms in the general industrial sector it also fell continuously from 1960 to 1980, and then leveled off during 1980–1984. The acid-test ratio showed a slight improvement in the consumer goods sector in 1970 as compared to 1965, ending in a higher value in 1984, while for firms in project management, it leveled off during 1970–1980 after falling during 1960–1970, and fell again modestly in 1984. The acid-test ratio fell during 1975–1984 in four out of the six industry groupings, while remaining virtually the same in the project management group during the same period. Only the consumer goods sector showed some improvements, but it, too, was lower when compared to its position back in 1960.

When we examine the ratio of net working capital to total assets in the six industry groupings of excellent firms, we find that the same trend was evident. In comparision to 1960, the ratio fell in all six groupings in 1984. The ratio fell most severely in project management (61.29 percent), followed by the consumer goods sector (36.58 percent) in this period. It fell continuously in high technology, while for the firms in project management it fell from 1960 to 1980, then leveled off in 1984. The slight improvement that was evident in the consumer goods and service sectors in 1975 as compared to 1970 dissipated again in 1980 and in 1984, while in the resourced-based sector it started to decline even from 1965. All this points to the deterioration of the liquidity positions of most of the excellent firms during the past twenty-five years of the period covered by our study.

When we compare the liquidity ratios of the control firms with those of the excellent firms, as shown in table 3.2, we find the same trend of declining ratios during 1960–1984 as was evident among the excellent firms. For the control firms, the current ratio in all six industry groupings fell in 1984 as compared to 1960, the decline being most severe and continuous for firms in the general industrial sector. For firms in the consumer goods sector, the ratio went up in 1975, then fell both in 1980 and 1984, while for firms in high technology, it fell almost continuously until 1980 and then leveled off in 1984. But for firms in the resource-based and service sectors, it declined in 1980 when compared to 1975, and then went up modestly in 1984. In all, the average for the control firms was slightly higher than the excellent firms both in 1960 and in 1984, and the decline was also slightly less severe for the control group than for the excellent group during 1960–1984.

The acid-test ratio of the control firms also fell in 1984 from the 1960 level for most of the groupings except project management, where, in fact, it rose slightly during this period. Again, the decline was most severe and continuous during 1960–1984 for firms in the general industrial group, followed by the resource-based sector. In contrast to the situation among the excellent firms, however, the control firms belonging to high technology and the consumer goods sectors, as well as the service and resource-based sectors, improved their positions in 1984 as compared to 1980, particularly in the resource-based sector where the ratio went up by 66 percent during the later years of our study. Also, the average percentage decline of the ratio for the control firms taken as a group was less than that of the ex-cellent firms as a group during the entire 1960–1984 period.

The ratio of net working capital to total assets also declined in all the industry groupings of the control firms during 1960–1984. Here, too, the fall of the ratio was highest in the general industrial sector, and it was almost continuous throughout the entire period. The ratio did improve dramatically for firms in project management both in 1975 and 1980 as compared to 1970, and it improved slightly for high technology firms in 1980, but it fell again in 1984 for both these groups. Only the service sector showed some improvements in 1984 as compared to 1980. The ratio fell off in the resource-based sector during the same period. In all, the average decline of this ratio during 1960–1984 was virtually the same for both the excellent and control firms.

It is, however, the growth of cash flow (net income plus all non-cash charges) that is the most important gauge of the financial condition of a firm. On Wall Street, cash flow has become the new gospel, although financial analysts are perhaps praising its revelatory power too loudly.[4] The cash generated by a company's operations is being hailed as a far more reliable barometer of financial health than the more traditional earning yardstick, which can be manipulated by different accounting practices. Just as the discrepancy between strong cash flow and lackluster earnings of a company reveals its unrealized potential, so also the healthy growth of cash flow and earnings indicate possibilities for further expansion and acquisition. Cash flow has become a real measure of a company's ability to finance itself and pay its obligations.

In table 3.3, we have shown the growth of cash flow of both the excellent and control firms during the later years of 1975–1984. We find that although the overall annual growth of the cash flow for the control firms was slightly lower than that of the excellent firms, the compound annual growth rate was higher in the consumer goods, general industrial, and service sectors among the control firms than it was in those sectors of the excellent firms during 1975–1984. For the control firms, it was higher in the general industrial and the resource-based sectors during the subperiod of 1975–1980, and in the consumer goods and service sectors during 1980–1984. Except for the decline in the growth of cash flow for firms in project management, which was precipitous during 1980–1984, the overall average compound annual growth of cash flow for the control firms during 1975–1984 was higher than that of the excellent firms. Nonetheless, the figures are quite close to each other when we take the entire decade into account.

## ASSET MANAGEMENT RATIOS OF THE EXCELLENT AND CONTROL FIRMS, 1960–1984

Asset management ratios or turnover ratios measure how effectively the firm is managing its assets. They try to answer the question of whether the total amount of each type of asset as reported in the balance sheet seems "reasonable" (i.e., too high or too low in view of the current and projected operating levels).[5] Here three ratios stand out foremost to measure the utilization of the assets of the company, namely, the inventory-turnover ratio, the asset-turnover ratio, and the fixed asset-turnover ratio. The inventory-turnover ratio is calculated by dividing the firm's average inventory into the cost of goods sold. The asset-turnover ratio is calculated by dividing the firm's total assets into sales. It indicates the efficiency with which the firm is able to use all of its assets to generate sales dollars. Finally, the fixed asset-turnover ratio measures the efficiency with which the firm has been using its *fixed* or earning assets to generate sales. It is calculated by dividing the firm's net fixed assets into annual net sales.

**Table 3.3**
**Average Annual Growth of Cash Flows of the Excellent and Control Firms, 1975-1984**

| Industry Groupings | Years | | |
|---|---|---|---|
| | 1975-1980 | 1980-1984 | 1975-1984 |
| A. Excellent Firms | | | |
| High Tech. | 22.25 | 12.75 | 13.71 |
| Consumer Goods | 14.94 | 3.61 | 9.76 |
| General Indus. | -0.81 | 25.30 | 10.04 |
| Service | 18.60 | 0.02 | 9.94 |
| Project Manage. | 28.60 | 9.10 | 19.54 |
| Resource-Based | 15.56 | 4.48 | 10.50 |
| Total | 13.40 | 9.68 | 11.73 |
| B. Control Firms | | | |
| High Tech. | 14.25 | 6.69 | 10.83 |
| Consumer Goods | 13.16 | 10.22 | 11.84 |
| General Indus. | 15.04 | 7.18 | 11.48 |
| Service | 10.23 | 14.70 | 12.19 |
| Project Manage. | 18.36 | -31.79 | -7.35 |
| Resource-Based | 21.40 | -3.43 | 9.66 |
| Total | 15.97 | 4.92 | 10.92 |

Source: Basic data were collected from Moody's Industrial Manuals,
        various issues covering 1960-1984.

In tables 3.4 and 3.5 we have calculated the three asset management ratios of the excellent and control firms, respectively, for the selected years covering 1960–1984. As is evident, the inventory-turnover ratio of the excellent firms increased from 1960 to 1984 in the general industrial and resource-based sectors, while it went down in the remaining four groupings. It increased for a short period for the firms in the high technology and the consumer goods sectors as well as in general industrial during 1980–1984, but fell in the service, project management, and resource-based sectors in the same period. The reason the ratio was so high in the service and project management sectors is that by the very nature of their business these industries possess very little inventory. The ratio, however, fell in 1984 in both these sectors when compared with the figures in 1960.

**Table 3.4**
**Turnover Ratios of the Excellent Firms for Selected Years, 1960–1984**

| Industry Groupings | Years | | | | | |
|---|---|---|---|---|---|---|
| | 1960 | 1965 | 1970 | 1975 | 1980 | 1984 |
| **A. Inventory-Turnover Ratios** | | | | | | |
| High Tech. | 5.26 | 3.85 | 4.69 | 3.56 | 3.76 | 4.54 |
| Consumer Goods | 3.43 | 3.38 | 2.79 | 3.03 | 2.97 | 3.38 |
| General Indus. | 4.47 | 4.80 | 4.83 | 3.78 | 4.27 | 5.32 |
| Service | 50.43 | 31.87 | 38.58 | 31.35 | 37.23 | 34.36 |
| Project Manage. | 16.77 | 52.32 | 24.31 | 22.76 | 19.95 | 12.41 |
| Resource-Based | 3.14 | 3.92 | 3.96 | 3.53 | 6.74 | 6.35 |
| **B. Asset-Turnover Ratios** | | | | | | |
| High Tech. | 1.74 | 1.73 | 1.45 | 1.40 | 1.50 | 1.47 |
| Consumer Goods | 1.72 | 1.66 | 1.45 | 1.52 | 1.52 | 1.42 |
| General Indus. | 1.24 | 1.34 | 1.19 | 1.25 | 1.26 | 1.21 |
| Service | 1.25 | 1.38 | 1.14 | 1.53 | 1.50 | 1.54 |
| Project Manage. | 2.76 | 2.23 | 1.57 | 2.23 | 2.24 | 1.19 |
| Resource-Based | 0.78 | 0.84 | 0.82 | 1.08 | 1.35 | 1.22 |
| **C. Fixed Asset-Turnover Ratios** | | | | | | |
| High Tech. | 2.87 | 3.62 | 2.57 | 2.69 | 2.74 | 2.27 |
| Consumer Goods | 3.88 | 3.77 | 3.27 | 3.54 | 3.37 | 2.58 |
| General Indus. | 2.18 | 2.44 | 1.82 | 1.97 | 2.17 | 1.92 |
| Service | 2.29 | 3.01 | 3.10 | 4.43 | 5.11 | 5.49 |
| Project Manage. | 7.28 | 13.14 | 3.91 | 3.69 | 3.26 | 2.08 |
| Resource-Based | 0.53 | 0.67 | 1.37 | 1.35 | 1.37 | 1.15 |

Source: Basic data were collected from Moody's Industrial Manuals,
various issues covering 1960-1984.

**Table 3.5**
**Turnover Ratios of the Control Firms for Selected Years, 1960–1984**

| Industry Groupings | Years | | | | | |
|---|---|---|---|---|---|---|
| | 1960 | 1965 | 1970 | 1975 | 1980 | 1984 |
| A. Inventory-Turnover Ratios | | | | | | |
| High Tech. | 4.16 | 3.45 | 3.14 | 3.49 | 3.76 | 4.55 |
| Consumer Goods | 6.32 | 6.50 | 5.35 | 4.73 | 4.93 | 5.23 |
| General Indus. | 4.33 | 3.96 | 3.70 | 3.97 | 4.92 | 7.05 |
| Service | 10.21 | 10.50 | 10.04 | 10.15 | 11.89 | 13.24 |
| Project Manage. | 5.95 | 10.41 | 6.73 | 5.02 | 4.99 | 9.24 |
| Resource-Based | 7.10 | 8.35 | 5.82 | 8.15 | 9.73 | 9.79 |
| B. Asset-Turnover Ratios | | | | | | |
| High Tech. | 1.59 | 1.66 | 1.47 | 1.61 | 1.59 | 1.68 |
| Consumer Goods | 2.00 | 1.83 | 1.73 | 1.82 | 1.93 | 1.81 |
| General Indus. | 1.04 | 1.03 | 1.00 | 1.27 | 1.39 | 1.30 |
| Service | 2.29 | 2.03 | 1.82 | 1.91 | 1.79 | 1.63 |
| Project Manage. | 2.39 | 2.39 | 1.78 | 1.73 | 1.59 | 1.76 |
| Resource-Based | 0.93 | 0.87 | 0.86 | 1.76 | 2.22 | 1.83 |
| C. Fixed Asset-Turnover Ratios | | | | | | |
| High Tech. | 6.47 | 5.81 | 4.07 | 4.33 | 4.46 | 4.30 |
| Consumer Goods | 4.49 | 3.47 | 3.16 | 4.11 | 4.67 | 4.03 |
| General Indus. | 2.14 | 1.99 | 1.83 | 2.27 | 2.57 | 2.40 |
| Service | 5.58 | 4.92 | 3.92 | 5.89 | 4.06 | 3.54 |
| Project Manage. | 4.71 | 5.15 | 2.49 | 2.41 | 2.99 | 2.97 |
| Resource-Based | 0.94 | 5.15 | 0.85 | 1.41 | 1.89 | 1.37 |

Source: Basic data were collected from Moody's Industrial Manuals, various issues covering 1960-1984.

In comparison, the asset-turnover ratio of the excellent firms decreased from 1960 to 1984 in four industry groupings and went up in only two groups during the same period. The drop during this period was most severe in the project management sector, while the gain was highest in the resource-based sector. In the 1980–1984 subperiod, all other groupings except the service sector witnessed a modest drop, after having shown a slight improvement in the previous subperiod 1975–1980. In 1984, the ratio was highest in the service sector, followed by the high technology sector.

The fixed asset-turnover ratio of the excellent firms was highest in the project management and service sectors, where fixed assets per dollar of sales are lower due to the nature of these industries. For the same reason, the ratio was lowest in the resource-based sector, which is generally capital-intensive and so generates fewer sales dollars per fixed asset. Here again, the ratio went down in 1984, as compared to 1960, in five of the six industry groupings. Only the service sector showed remarkable improvement during this entire period. Also, the ratio went down in all of the same five groupings during 1980–1984, as compared to 1975–1980. Thus the trend that was evident in many other ratios was also present here (i.e., the majority of the ratios went down during 1960–1984 for the excellent firms).

Table 3.5 shows these three types of asset management ratios for the control firms for the same six selected periods covering 1960–1984. The inventory-turnover ratio in the five industry groupings (except consumer goods) had gone up in 1984 when compared to that of 1960. Also, the ratio went up for all the groupings during 1980–1984—a situation markedly different from that in the excellent firms, where the ratio in three groupings out of the six had deteriorated. For the control firms, however, the situation had improved even before 1980, since improvement in the high technology, consumer goods, general industrial, service, and resource-based sectors started right after 1975, when the U.S. economy was emerging from the deepest post-World War II recession.

With respect to the asset-turnover ratio of the control firms, the result was mixed. During 1960–1984 the ratio went up in three industry groupings but it went down in the remaining three groupings. This was still a slightly better situation when compared to the asset-turnover ratio of the excellent firms, where the ratio declined in four of the six groupings during the same period. Again, the ratio went up in two groupings among control firms during 1980–1984, while it increased in only one group among the excellent firms. When we compare the average value of the asset-turnover ratio of these two groups of firms we find that here, too, the average ratios among the control firms in 1960 and 1984, respectively, were 1.71 and1.67, while for the excellent firms the ratios were 1.58 and 1.34.

A similarly positive situation for the control firms is evident in the case of the fixed asset-turnover ratio, where we find that for the control firms the ratio went up in two industry groupings from 1960 to 1984, but in only one grouping among the excellent firms during the same period. Although this ratio deteriorated for both the groups during 1980–1984, it went up clearly in five industry groupings among the control firms during 1975–1980. Among the excellent firms the ratio increased in only three industry groupings during the same time period. Again, for the control firms, the average fixed asset-turnover ratio was about 28 percent higher than the excellent firms in 1960, while it was 20 percent higher than the excellent firms in 1984. Overall, the asset management of the control firms was better than the excellent firms during the twenty-five-year period covered by our study.

Professor Edward I. Altman was the first to use the technique of multiple discriminant analysis, with the help of financial ratios, to predict the weakening position of a company and its eventual bankruptcy.[6] Altman developed a simple equation that has been useful in evaluating performance and predicting the potential bankruptcy of a firm. The equation is as follows:

$$Z = 1.2X_1 + 1.4X_2 + 3.3X_3 + .6X_4 + 1.0X_5$$

where

$Z$ = A score that indicates the financial strength (high value) or weakness (low value of the company concerned;

$X_1$ = net working capital divided by total assets;

$X_2$ = retained earnings divided by total assets;

$X_3$ = earnings before interest and taxes (EBIT) divided by total assets;

$X_4$ = market value of common and preferred stocks divided by total assets;

$X_5$ = sales divided by total assets.

In his study of manufacturing companies, Altman found that the $Z$ scores frequently predicted bankruptcy.[7] Companies with $Z$ scores above 3.0 were found to be healthy, while those with scores below 1.8 generally went bankrupt within one year. Companies with $Z$ scores between 1.8 and 3.0 fall within a gray area where survival is not certain. Although Altman calculated the $Z$ scores mainly for U.S. manufacturing companies, the analysis is also useful for other types of industries, as other studies have proven. In general, while the absolute $Z$ score is important for indicating the degree of financial distress or security of a firm, the trend in Z scores is more important than a single score in gauging the future financial health of the firm concerned. The important thing is to measure Z over a period of time.[8]

In table 3.6, we have calculated Altman's Z scores for twenty-five "truly" excellent firms, which, according to Peters and Waterman, passed all the tests for 1975, 1980, and 1984, respectively.

We find that during 1975–1984, the Z score went down for fifteen companies, went up for eight firms, and remained virtually the same for the other two firms. Compared with the 1975 figures, it declined in 1980 and again in 1984 for seven firms, while it went up in 1980 and again in 1984 for only two firms. In 1975, the Z score was highest for Merck (8.21), and above 6.0 for Digital Equipment, Emerson Electric, K-Mart, 3M, and Wal-Mart. But Z scores for all these companies went down in 1984. In 1984, the Z score was highest for Bristol-Myers (7.2) and none other was higher than 6.0. Evidently the Z score deteriorated for the majority of these excellent firms during the period covered by our analysis. Ten of these twenty-five companies had a Z score below 3.0, thereby indicating cause for concern about liquidity and performance. The lowest score in 1984 was for Fluor Corporation (1.9), only slightly above 1.8 and therefore in a dangerous situation.

## OPERATING EFFICIENCY OF THE EXCELLENT AND CONTROL FIRMS

The operating efficiency of a firm refers to how efficiently the firm produces the products it sells. The main thrust here is to measure the cost-effectiveness of the firm: whether it is maintaining the product quality at minimum or reasonably competitive cost. Although there are many ways of evaluating the cost-effectiveness of a firm, operating efficiency is generally measured by the ratio of the firm, by sales and net income per employee, and the sales and net income per dollar of plants and equipment.[9] All this has a clear bearing on the earnings and profitability of a company, as they are directly affected by the way a firm conducts its usual business in a competitive environment.

Table 3.7 shows the average annual compound growth rate of gross plants and equipment of both the excellent and control firms for the years covering 1975–1984. For the excellent firms during the period 1975–1980, the average annual growth rate was highest among firms in project management. They also maintained the lead in the other two time periods. Although the resource-based sector was almost identical in growth rate to project management in 1975–1980, it fell to the fifth place during 1980–1984,

**Table 3.6**
**Altman's Z Scores for 25 Excellent Firms, 1975–1984**

| Name of the Excellent Firm | Altman's Z Score | | |
|---|---|---|---|
| | 1975 | 1980 | 1984 |
| Amdahl | NMF* | 4.08 | 2.78 |
| Boeing | 5.94 | 3.30 | 2.81 |
| Bristol Meyers | 4.06 | 7.55 | 7.20 |
| Caterpillar Tractor | 4.53 | 3.96 | 2.43 |
| Chesebrough-Pond's | 3.12 | 4.30 | 5.19 |
| Dana Corp. | 3.59 | 3.01 | 4.11 |
| Data General | 2.80 | 2.80 | 2.30 |
| Delta Airlines | 2.61 | 3.10 | 2.48 |
| Digital Equipment | 6.51 | 4.72 | 4.39 |
| Dow Chemical | 3.17 | 2.46 | 2.44 |
| Du Pont | 3.54 | 3.78 | 3.07 |
| Emerson Electric | 6.91 | 5.59 | 4.58 |
| Fluor | 4.46 | 5.24 | 1.90 |
| I.B.M. | 2.20 | 2.20 | 2.80 |
| K-Mart | 6.90 | 3.80 | 3.64 |
| Levi Strauss | 3.90 | 5.70 | 4.50 |
| Marriott | 2.15 | 2.75 | 2.42 |
| Maytag | 4.91 | 5.18 | 5.27 |
| McDonald's | 2.32 | 2.90 | 2.30 |
| Merck | 8.21 | 6.26 | 4.54 |
| Minnesota Mining | 6.02 | 5.85 | 5.99 |
| Revlon | 5.11 | 3.29 | 3.77 |
| Standard Oil(Ind.)/Amoco | 3.65 | 4.25 | 3.87 |
| Texas Instruments | 3.90 | 2.90 | 3.10 |
| Wal-Mart | 7.50 | 5.18 | 4.04 |

\* NMF — Not meaningful due to losses in the initial terminal
        year of this study.

Source: Basic data were collected from Moody's Industrial Manuals,
        various issues covering 1960-1984.

**Table 3.7**

**Average Annual Growth of Gross Plants and Equipment of the Excellent Firms, 1975-1984**

| Industry Groupings | Years | | |
|---|---|---|---|
| | 1975-1980 | 1980-1984 | 1975-1984 |
| A. Excellent Firms | | | |
| High Tech. | 9.60 | 9.91 | 9.74 |
| Consumer Goods | 12.25 | 10.83 | 11.62 |
| General Indus. | 11.58 | 7.06 | 9.55 |
| Service | 11.25 | 15.78 | 13.24 |
| Project Manage. | 17.57 | 19.77 | 18.54 |
| Resource-Based | 17.56 | 9.39 | 13.86 |
| Total | 13.62 | 9.65 | 11.84 |
| B. Control Firms | | | |
| High Tech. | 6.36 | 3.24 | 4.96 |
| Consumer Goods | 13.22 | 7.28 | 10.54 |
| General Indus. | 5.04 | 9.86 | 7.16 |
| Service | 11.49 | 1.63 | 6.99 |
| Project Manage. | 9.73 | -1.84 | 4.43 |
| Resource-Based | 12.49 | 9.92 | 11.34 |
| Total | 9.95 | 7.52 | 8.86 |

Source: Basic data were collected from Moody's Industrial Manuals, various issues covering 1960-1984.

with the service sector occupying the second position in that period. For the entire decade covering 1975-1984, however, the resource-based sector was second in growth rate of plants and equipment, with the service sector occupying the third place. Surprisingly, the high technology sector held the last place during 1975-1980, and the fifth place during the entire period 1975-1984. Also, the overall average growth rate of plants and equipment fell by 13 percent from 1975 to 1984.

Among the control firms, the highest average growth rate of plants and equipment was obtained by firms in the consumer goods sector during 1975-1980. The resource-based sector maintained a strong position during 1975-1980, but was the first in growth rate for the whole decade of 1975-1984. Interestingly, among the control firms, the high technology sector was quite low in growth of plants and equipment as was true in

the case of the excellent firms. The negative number for the project management sector during 1980–1984 could be due to the very small sample of only two firms. Overall, the average annual growth of plants and equipment
among the control firms was lower than among the excellent firms in all
the selected years, although the percentage decline of the growth rate was
higher for the excellent firms than the control firms during 1975–1984.

The operating ratio in table 3.8 for both the excellent and control firms
was calculated by dividing net sales into the cost of goods sold. It thus
renders the reciprocal of the gross profit margin. Therefore, the lower
the ratio, the higher the operating efficiency of the company. Here we
find that, for the excellent firms, the ratio went down during 1975–1984
in only two industry groupings while it went up in the remaining four groupings. However, during 1975–1980 as well as during 1980–1984, the ratio
declined in three industry groupings. For the entire decade, the worst decline

**Table 3.8**
**Operating Ratios of the Excellent and Control Firms for Selected Years, 1975–1984**

| Industry Groupings | Years | | | Percentage Change, 1975–80 | Percentage Change, 1980–84 | Percentage Change, 1975–1984 |
|---|---|---|---|---|---|---|
| | 1975 | 1980 | 1984 | | | |
| A. Excellent Firms | | | | | | |
| High Tech. | 0.671 | 0.625 | 0.647 | -0.68 | 3.52 | -3.58 |
| Consumer Goods | 0.545 | 0.541 | 0.522 | -0.73 | -3.51 | -4.22 |
| General Indus. | 0.744 | 0.769 | 0.781 | 3.36 | 1.56 | 4.97 |
| Service | 0.764 | 0.783 | 0.776 | 2.48 | -0.89 | 1.57 |
| Project Manage. | 0.952 | 0.920 | 0.958 | -3.36 | 4.13 | 0.63 |
| Resource-Based | 0.600 | 0.631 | 0.619 | 5.17 | -1.90 | 3.17 |
| B. Control Firms | | | | | | |
| High TEch. | 0.667 | 0.711 | 0.701 | 6.19 | -1.41 | 4.85 |
| Consumer Goods | 0.635 | 0.634 | 0.582 | -0.16 | -8.20 | -8.35 |
| General Indus. | 0.796 | 0.797 | 0.809 | 0.12 | 1.63 | 1.63 |
| Service | 0.736 | 0.718 | 0.683 | -2.45 | -4.87 | -7.20 |
| Project Manage. | 0.915 | 0.832 | 0.906 | -9.07 | 8.89 | -0.98 |
| Resource-Based | 0.726 | 0.735 | 0.709 | 1.38 | -3.54 | -2.34 |

Source: Basic data were collected from Moody's Industrial Manuals,
various issues covering 1960–1984.

took place in the consumer goods sector, followed by firms in high technology, while the highest growth of the ratio occurred in general industrial, followed by the resource-based sector.

When we compare this ratio for the excellent firms with that of the control firms, we find that the former group did better than the latter group, as the ratio went down in four out of the six industry groupings among the control firms during 1975–1984. The decline was highest in the consumer goods sector, followed by the service sector, but the ratio went up significantly only in the high technology sector in this period. Also, the performance of the control firms was superior during the two subperiods, when it went down for three industry groupings during 1975–1980 and in four groupings during 1980–1984. Although the average operating ratio for the control firms was somewhat higher than the average of the excellent firms both in 1975 and 1984, this ratio—which should be going down to reflect the increasing operating efficiency—actually went up slightly for the excellent firms, while it went down, also slightly, for the control firms during the decade of 1975–1984.

In table 3.9 we have calculated the sales and net income per employee of both the excellent and control firms for the years 1975 and 1984, respectively. This table reveals the fact that sales per employee were much higher for the control firms in the high technology, consumer goods, and general industrial sectors in both 1975 and 1984, while it was higher in the project management and resource-based sectors for the excellent firms in both 1975 and 1984, with the service sector being higher only in 1984 for the control firms. But when we examine the percentage change of sales per employee for these two groups of firms between 1975 and 1984, we find that except for the service sector, the percentage increase was higher for the other excellent firms in five groupings. Interestingly, the highest sales per employee in 1975 as well as in 1984 were enjoyed by the resource-based sector in both the excellent and control firms. Obviously, the relatively higher price of oil generated much higher revenues for these oil-based companies in both groups during the period covered by our study.

But when we look into the net income per employee, we find that the excellent firms were superior to the control firms in all six industry groupings, both in 1975 and 1984. Also, the percentage changes for the excellent firms during 1975–1984 were positive in all the groupings except general industrial, while they were negative in general industrial and the project management sectors for the control firms during the same period. In both 1975 and 1984, the average net income per employee in the excellent firms was highest in the consumer goods sector, which was also highest among the control firms in 1984, while the general industrial

**Table 3.9**
**Sales and Net Income per Employee of the Excellent and Control Firms, 1975-1984**

| Industry | Sales Per Employee ($) | | | Net Income Per Employee ($) | | |
|---|---|---|---|---|---|---|
| Groupings | 1975 | 1984 | Percent Change, 1975-84 | 1975 | 1984 | Percent Change, 1975-84 |
| A. Excellent Firms | | | | | | |
| High Tech. | 31,492.86 | 73,448.51 | 133.22 | 2,143.81 | 5,348.09 | 149.47 |
| Consumer Goods | 48,792.74 | 94,335.00 | 93.34 | 4,465.38 | 6,999.17 | 56.74 |
| General Indus. | 46,653.33 | 94,056.67 | 101.61 | 3,115.00 | 2,978.33 | -4.39 |
| Service | 33,677.14 | 62,032.86 | 84.20 | 1,421.29 | 3.448.57 | 142.64 |
| Project Manage. | 66,370.00 | 122,190.00 | 84.10 | 1,980.00 | 4,245.50 | 114.42 |
| Resource-Based | 220,018.00 | 410,526.00 | 86.59 | 12,232.00 | 22,498.00 | 83.93 |
| B. Control Firms | | | | | | |
| High Tech. | 34,381.43 | 77,886.19 | 126.54 | 1,805.76 | 4,182.76 | 131.63 |
| Consumer Goods | 58,034.62 | 108,642.31 | 87.20 | 2,975.38 | 6,968.46 | 134.20 |
| General Indus. | 76,323.33 | 120,951.67 | 58.47 | 3,356.67 | 1,162.01 | -65.38 |
| Service | 33,662.86 | 78,975.71 | 134.46 | 707.43 | 2,734.28 | 286.51 |
| Project Manage. | 47,995.00 | 73,420.00 | 52.97 | 1,695.00 | 185.00 | -89.08 |
| Resource-Based | 206,880.00 | 309,786.00 | 49.74 | 9,086.00 | 13,508.00 | 48.67 |

Source: Basic data were collected from Moody's Industrial Manuals, various issues covering 1960-1984.

grouping was second among the excellent firms but first among the control firms in 1975. However, both the service and consumer goods sectors among the control firms surpassed those among the excellent firms in percentage growth in these years. Service and consumer goods also enjoyed the highest growth rates in all the groupings of both the excellent and control firms during 1975-1984.

When we calculate the sales per dollar of gross plant and equipment of these two groups of firms during 1975-1984, as shown in table 3.10, we find that here, too, the control firms on average did slightly better than the excellent firms. For the former group, the figures declined in three of the six groupings in 1984 as compared to 1975, while the figures went down in all the groupings among the excellent firms, except in the service sector where it went up by 19 percent during the same period. Also, among the excellent firms, sales per dollar value of gross plant and equipment were highest in the service sector both in 1975 and 1984. This was

**Table 3.10**
**Sales and Net Income per Dollar of Gross Plants and Equipment of the Excellent and Control Firms, 1975–1984**

| Industry Groupings | Sales per $ of Gross Plant & Equipment | | | Net Income per $ of Gross Plant & Equipment | | |
|---|---|---|---|---|---|---|
| | 1975 | 1984 | % Change | 1975 | 1984 | % Change |
| | | A. Excellent Firms | | | | |
| High Tech. | 2.71 | 2.25 | -16.97 | 0.19 | 0.16 | -15.79 |
| Consumer Goods | 3.53 | 2.59 | -26.63 | 0.26 | 0.16 | -38.46 |
| General Indus. | 1.97 | 1.43 | -27.41 | 0.13 | 0.10 | -23.08 |
| Service | 4.58 | 5.48 | 19.65 | 0.13 | 0.20 | 53.85 |
| Project Manage. | 3.68 | 2.08 | -43.48 | 0.11 | 0.11 | 0.00 |
| Resource-Based | 1.35 | 1.16 | -14.07 | 0.08 | 0.06 | -25.00 |
| | | B. Control Firms | | | | |
| High Tech. | 3.55 | 3.91 | 10.14 | 0.09 | 0.17 | 88.89 |
| Consumer Goods | 4.06 | 4.32 | 6.40 | 0.19 | 0.21 | 10.53 |
| General Indus. | 3.63 | 2.39 | -34.16 | 0.48 | 0.25 | -47.92 |
| Service | 5.10 | 3.61 | -29.22 | 0.42 | 0.15 | -64.29 |
| Project Manage. | 2.66 | 3.36 | 26.32 | 0.06 | 0.03 | -50.00 |
| Resource-Based | 1.41 | 1.37 | -2.83 | 0.06 | 0.06 | 0.00 |

Source: Basic data were collected from Moody's Industrial Manuals, various issues covering 1960-1984.

true for the control firms in 1975 but not in 1984, when the figure was highest in the consumer goods sector. It is to be noted here that the lowest figure in both 1975 and 1984 belonged to the resource-based sector in both groups. Obviously, sales per dollar of gross plant and equipment would be relatively low for an industry group marked by a capital-intensive production process.

When we compare the net income per dollar of gross plant and equipment for the two kinds of firms during 1975–1984, the result is almost the same as in our other comparisons because here, too, the control firms did slightly better than the excellent firms. The figure went down from 1975 to 1984 in three groupings among the control firms, while it went down in four groupings among the excellent firms. Among the excellent firms, it was highest in the consumer goods sector in 1975 and in the service sector in 1984. Among the control firms, however, the highest place was occupied by the general industrial sector in both 1975 and 1984. When we compute the average value for both control and excellent firms,

**Table 3.11**

**Ranking of 36 Excellent Firms by Sales and Net Income per Employee, and Sales and Net Income per Dollar of Gross Plant and Equipment, 1984**

| Name of the Excellent Firm | Ranking By | | | | |
|---|---|---|---|---|---|
| | Sales per Employee | Net Income per Employee | Sales per $ of Gross Plant and Equipment | Net Income per $ of Gross Plant and Equipment | Overall Ranking Average |
| | (1) | (2) | (3) | (4) | (5) |
| Amdahl | 28 | 39 | 82 | 73 | 55 |
| Avon | 57 | 40 | 49 | 36 | 45 |
| Boeing | 29 | 20 | 51 | 26 | 31 |
| Bristol-Myers | 25 | 13 | 33 | 7 | 19 |
| Caterpillar | 31 | 103 | 95 | 79 | 77 |
| Chesebrough-Pond's | 74 | 44 | 24 | 19 | 40 |
| Dana Corp. | 39 | 38 | 41 | 38 | 39 |
| Data General | 85 | 41 | 66 | 39 | 58 |
| Delta Airlines | 105 | 42 | 78 | 75 | 75 |
| Digital Equipment | 87 | 97 | 59 | 6 | 62 |
| Disney Productions | 32 | 71 | 2 | 8 | 28 |
| Dow Chemical | 104 | 16 | 97 | 89 | 76 |
| Du Pont | 7 | 17 | 89 | 86 | 50 |
| Eastman Kodak | 51 | 40 | 100 | 69 | 65 |
| Emerson Electric | 73 | 29 | 39 | 16 | 39 |
| Fluor Corp. | 16 | 100 | 86 | 104 | 76 |
| Hewlett-Packard | 72 | 21 | 68 | 18 | 45 |
| Intel | 93 | 31 | 92 | 51 | 67 |
| IBM | 24 | 6 | 81 | 21 | 33 |
| Johnson & Johnson | 55 | 27 | 61 | 53 | 49 |
| K-Mart | 32 | 70 | 2 | 8 | 28 |
| Levi Strauss | 82 | 89 | 15 | 96 | 70 |
| Marriott | 103 | 88 | 72 | 70 | 83 |
| Maytag | 35 | 14 | 50 | 20 | 30 |
| McDonald's | 68 | 51 | 40 | 58 | 54 |
| Merck | 97 | 25 | 93 | 33 | 62 |
| Minnesota Mining | 45 | 19 | 77 | 34 | 44 |
| National Semiconductor | 102 | 85 | 76 | 77 | 85 |
| Procter & Gamble | 15 | 11 | 70 | 46 | 35 |
| Raychem | 76 | 49 | 79 | 59 | 66 |
| Revlon | 63 | 56 | 47 | 48 | 53 |
| Schlumberger | 31 | 5 | 94 | 25 | 39 |
| Standard Oil (Ind.) /Amoco | 4 | 1 | 98 | 72 | 44 |
| Texas Instruments | 84 | 23 | 63 | 52 | 56 |
| Wal-Mart | 94 | 75 | 1 | 4 | 43 |
| Wang Laboratories | 81 | 96 | 66 | 15 | 64 |

we find that both sales and net income per dollar of gross plant and equipment were slightly higher among the control firms in both 1975 and 1984. Our analysis also reveals, however, that capital productivity in both these groups went down during 1975–1984, although the deterioration was more severe for the majority of the excellent firm groupings than for their counterparts among the control firms.

In table 3.11, we have ranked the 36 publicly held excellent firms listed by Peters and Waterman as having passed all their tests of excellence. For our total sample of 108 firms (54 excellent and 54 control firms), we have ranked them by the four statistics of operating efficiency, namely; sales per employee, net income per employee, sales per dollar of gross plant and equipment, and net income per dollar of gross plant and equipment. Only 13 of the excellent firms ranked within the top 36 firms in terms of sales per employee. Similarly, only 15 excellent firms ranked within the top 36 firms in terms of net income per employee. But when we rank the firms in terms of sales per dollar of gross plant and equipment, the number of excellent firms in the top 36 is only slightly higher—16 to be exact. The situation is still worse when companies are ranked by net income per dollar of gross plant and equipment. In this case, only 6 excellent firms qualified to be included among the top 36 firms.

The overall average ranking was also disappointing for these 36 excellent public firms, as table 3.11 shows. Only 7 of these firms outranked all others—in terms of the four efficiency tests—to be included in this list of 36 firms. Among all the so-called excellent firms, only Boeing, Bristol-Myers, Disney Productions, IBM, K-Mart, Maytag, and Procter & Gamble companies belonged among the top 36 firms in terms of the overall ranking average as composed of the 108 firms. A so-called excellent company such as Standard Oil of Indiana (Amoco) ranked fourth and first in terms of sales per employee and net income per employee, respectively, but fell among the lowest 30 percent in terms of sales and net income per dollar of gross plant and equipment, to be ranked, on average, much lower than the top 36. Similarly, Wal-Mart ranked number one and four in sales and net income per dollar of gross plant and equipment, respectively, but fell in the lowest 30 percent in terms of sales and net income per employee. Not a single excellent firm was among the top ten in terms of the average of these four efficiency measures, and only one, Bristol-Myers, barely qualified to be among the top 20 firms in average of rankings. Overall, less than 20 percent of the 36 excellent firms surpassed others in these efficiency tests among all the 108 firms of our sample.

## NOTES

1. Joseph Bradley, *Administrative Financial Management* (Hinsdale, Ill.: The Dryden Press, 1974), pp. 56–60.

2. Edward Altman, "Financial Ratios, Discriminant Analysis, and the Prediction of Corporate Bankruptcy," *Journal of Finance*, Vol. 23 (Sept. 1968): 589–609.

3. Fred Weston and Eugene Brigham, *Managerial Finance* (Hinsdale, Ill.: The Dryden Press, 1984) 7th ed., pp. 159–60.

4. Elizabeth Kaplan, "Wall Street Zeros in on Cash Flows," *Dun's Business Monthly* (July 1985): 40–41.

5. Eugene Brigham, *Fundamentals of Financial Management* (Hinsdale, Ill.: The Dryden Press, 1989), 5th ed., pp. 268–71.

6. Edward Altman, "Financial Ratios," pp. 593–98.

7. Edward Altman, *Financial Distress* (New York: John Wiley & Sons, 1983).

8. Edward Altman and Joseph Spivack, "Predicting Bankruptcy: The *Value Line* Relative Financial Strength vs. the Zeta Bankruptcy Classification Approach," *Financial Analysts' Journal*, Vol. 39 (Nov.-Dec. 1983): pp. 60–67.

9. Frederick Amling, *Investments* (Englewood Cliffs, N.J.: Prentice-Hall, 1984), pp. 405–6.

# 4

# Capital Structure and Valuation Analysis of the United States' Excellent Firms

There is a great deal of controversy in the finance literature about the role of capital structure in the valuation of a firm.[1] In their celebrated article, Franco Modigliani and Merton Miller demonstrated that under certain assumptions such as the absence of taxes, transaction expenses, and bankruptcy costs, the market value of a firm is independent of its capital structure.[2] More recently, Miller has argued that the introduction of corporate and personal taxes does not alter the irrelevance of capital structure in the absence of bankruptcy costs.[3] To him, there is no such thing as an optimal debt-equity ratio for any single firm. The market is interested only in the total amount of debt, and no single firm can influence that.

There are many others, however, who have argued that because of the absence of bankruptcy costs, and the tax deductibility of interest payments, capital structure will affect the value of a firm. [4] At present, debt financing is the cheapest way for a company to obtain capital. A heavy reliance on debt financing tends to raise the rate of return to the common stockholders, provided the fund is invested suitably and at a higher rate than the interest paid for using them. This process of borrowing money at a lower rate and investing it at a higher rate is referred to as *trading on the equity*. But a larger debt also creates a higher degree of financial leverage, and if the revenue of the company is unstable, it will create more instability in the earnings per share. As Amling has pointed out, if a company experiences a wide fluctuation of earnings because of its revenue patterns, it will go through an even wider and more unstable fluctuation in earnings if there is a large amount of debt in the equity structure.[5]

Most financial economists, along with the textbook authors on the subject, believe that there is an optimum capital structure that will maximize the value of a firm at a given time.[6] By its mix of debt and equity, the firm may minimize its average cost of capital and maximize its value by a judicious process of trade-off between the tax shields of debt and the costs of bankruptcy. Debt in the capital structure increases the risk of loss to the common stockholders, and because of the additional risk, the price-earnings ratio of common stock is generally lowered. But at the *optimum* debt level, the percentage drop of the price-earnings ratio is less than the tax advantage, thereby increasing the value of the firm. Thus, an analysis of the role of debt and the debt-equity ratio is essential to determine the optimal capital structure of a firm.

## NATURE OF CAPITAL STRUCTURE OF THE EXCELLENT FIRMS

The source of capital should enhance the value of a firm in the long run. Capital structure is simply the sum of the net worth plus long-term debt. Thus the composition of capital—long-term debt, preferred stock, common stock (par value plus capital surplus), and retained earnings—should reflect the ability of the firm in question to undertake improvements in production facilities and to expand the product mix, which in turn, should boost the earnings per share of the company and the value of its stocks in the market place. As long-term debt provides a tax shield, and should be incorporated in the capital structure, so also does it increase the risk of potential bankruptcy. Thus, *ceteris paribus*, the lower the long-term debt in the capital structure, the better off the company is in the long run. Similarly, the larger the share of common stock and retained earnings, the more suited the firm will be to maximize the stockholders' wealth.

In table 4.1, we have estimated the capital structure of the excellent firms from 1960 to 1984. The table shows that in 1960, the percentage of long-term debt to total capital was highest in the service sector, followed by the high technology sector. It decreased significantly from 1960 to 1984 for both these groupings, but in absolute terms the debt figure increased fifteen-fold for the service sector and ten-fold for the high technology group. Obviously, these two industries, being relatively new, had a much greater need for external capital at the pioneering stage of development. Later on, as those industries matured, they relied more on internal capital in the form of retained earnings. The percentage decline of long-term debt to total capital was also significant in project management, although this percentage varied quite a bit in the different subperiods. Again, this variability is probably due to the fact that we are dealing with an extremely small sample of two firms only. But when we look into the increase of long-term debt in total capital, from 1960 to 1984, we find it to be highest in the general industrial sector, followed by the resource-based sector, and then by the consumer goods sector. These are the industries that are more mature and less growth-oriented in our economy. It is interesting to note that the role of preferred stock in capital structure was miniscule in all these industrial groupings, as issuing preferred stock does not offer any tax advantage. It is only a temporary avenue for raising funds, or a vehicle for funding friendly acquisitions—a phenomenon we witness in the general corporate structure across industries.

When we examine the growth of common stockholders' equity in the capital structure of the excellent firms, we find that except in the service sector and in project management, retained earnings were the main source of capital in all industry groupings in 1960. Retained earnings increased dramatically by 1984, in percentage terms particularly, and all sectors showed tremendous growth in absolute terms. From 1960 to 1984, growth was over 70 percent in the high technology, consumer goods, and resource-based sectors, and close to 50 percent in the other three groupings. This indicates that in all these industries internal financing has become the prime source of capital expansion. However, the percent of common stock (par value plus capital surplus) in the capital structure fell in all six industry groupings during 1960–1984, most dramatically in project management. Because of the potential dilution of ownership and the depressing effect on the current stock prices entailed by this drop, project management was not the most popular choice among these firms during the last twenty-five years covered by our study.

When we compare the components of capital structure in the control firms with those of the excellent firms, as shown in table 4.2, we find that the proportion of long-term debt had gone up in 1984, from 1960, in five of the six industry groupings, while it dipped slightly in the remaining one during the same period. The percentage of long-term debt in total capital grew most in the resource-based sector and general industrial sector—two of the slower-growing sectors of the general economy. It grew the least in the high technology sector during 1960–1984, because high technology was marked by a faster rate of growth during the last two decades. Here, also, the proportion and the rate of growth of the preferred stock were negligible for most of the groupings, except for project management where it grew significantly during 1960–1984.

The growth of retained earnings in the capital structure of the control firms was mixed during 1960–1984. In percentage terms, retained earnings grew in three of the six industry groupings, while they fell in the

**Table 4.1**
**Composition of Capital Structure of the Excellent Firms, 1960–1984**

| Types of Capital | Years | | | | | | | | | | | |
|---|---|---|---|---|---|---|---|---|---|---|---|---|
| | 1960 | | 1965 | | 1970 | | 1975 | | 1980 | | 1984 | |
| | $Mill. | % | $Mill. | % | $Mill. | % | $Mill. | % | $Mill. | % | $Mill. | % |
| **A. High Technology** | | | | | | | | | | | | |
| L-T Debt | 1,163.9 | 23.35 | 1,564.6 | 17.72 | 4,787.5 | 25.34 | 7,662.7 | 22.25 | 9,593.4 | 16.42 | 11,530.1 | 12.06 |
| Pf. Stock | 87.4 | 1.68 | 101.4 | 1.15 | 75.3 | 0.40 | 323.2 | 0.94 | 1,265.8 | 2.16 | 983.8 | 1.03 |
| Com. Stock | 1,621.8 | 31.16 | 2,172.7 | 24.60 | 4,369.0 | 23.12 | 6,789.7 | 19.71 | 8,816.5 | 15.09 | 14,197.1 | 14.85 |
| Ret. Earn. | 2,332.4 | 44.81 | 4,991.6 | 56.53 | 9,663.3 | 56.14 | 19,667.8 | 57.10 | 38,758.1 | 66.33 | 68,901.5 | 72.06 |
| **B. Consumer Goods** | | | | | | | | | | | | |
| L-T Debt | 227.8 | 8.95 | 284.3 | 7.31 | 990.3 | 12.48 | 1,985.0 | 14.53 | 2,850.1 | 11.74 | 4,323.2 | 12.68 |
| Pf Stock | 26.5 | 1.04 | 16.2 | 0.41 | 21.6 | 0.28 | 39.8 | 0.29 | 286.3 | 1.18 | 54.4 | 0.16 |
| Com. Stock | 842.9 | 33.13 | 1,147.3 | 29.49 | 1,543.2 | 19.86 | 1,801.4 | 13.19 | 2,054.9 | 8.47 | 3,234.7 | 9.49 |
| Ret. Earn. | 1,447.4 | 56.88 | 2,442.9 | 62.79 | 5,236.9 | 67.38 | 9,836.3 | 71.99 | 19,079.1 | 78.61 | 26,470.8 | 77.67 |
| **C. General Industrial** | | | | | | | | | | | | |
| L-T Debt | 1,535.5 | 20.02 | 1,972.7 | 17.73 | 2,390.0 | 16.69 | 4,774.6 | 21.72 | 8,467.1 | 24.37 | 16,220.6 | 33.94 |
| Pf. Stock | 310.1 | 4.04 | 290.6 | 2.61 | 294.4 | 2.06 | 289.8 | 1.32 | 684.2 | 1.97 | 465.7 | 0.98 |
| Com. Stock | 695.0 | 9.06 | 755.3 | 6.79 | 809.2 | 5.65 | 926.6 | 4.22 | 1,084.1 | 3.12 | 1,606.9 | 3.34 |
| Ret. Earns. | 5,130.1 | 66.88 | 8,101.1 | 72.85 | 10,824.8 | 75.60 | 15,985.8 | 72.74 | 24,510.1 | 70.54 | 29,775.8 | 61.94 |

## D. Service

| | | | | | | | | | | | |
|---|---|---|---|---|---|---|---|---|---|---|---|
| L-T Debt | 390.0 | 47.77 | 435.0 | 40.30 | 1,204.3 | 46.07 | 1,805.0 | 35.35 | 2,982.2 | 30.48 | 6,043.8 | 36.43 |
| Pf. Stock | 7.5 | 0.92 | 2.1 | 0.20 | 3.3 | 0.13 | 8.6 | 0.16 | 119.7 | 1.22 | 273.2 | 1.65 |
| Com. Stock | 137.7 | 16.87 | 197.4 | 18.30 | 554.6 | 21.22 | 1,514.4 | 29.02 | 1,801.5 | 18.41 | 2,237.1 | 13.48 |
| Ret. Earn. | 281.2 | 34.44 | 444.7 | 41.20 | 851.5 | 32.58 | 1,851.6 | 35.47 | 4,881.2 | 49.89 | 8,036.3 | 48.44 |

## E. Project Management

| | | | | | | | | | | | |
|---|---|---|---|---|---|---|---|---|---|---|---|
| L-T Debt | 70.5 | 21.76 | 98.3 | 19.49 | 640.3 | 40.52 | 147.3 | 9.71 | 155.5 | 5.12 | 1,008.8 | 14.91 |
| Pf. Stock | .... | .... | .... | .... | 0.9 | 0.06 | 13.9 | 0.98 | 0.9 | 0.01 | 348.2 | 5.14 |
| Com. Stock | 135.5 | 41.80 | 153.2 | 30.36 | 523.2 | 32.12 | 572.3 | 40.50 | 932.4 | 30.70 | 1,959.9 | 28.96 |
| Ret. Earn. | 118.1 | 36.44 | 253.2 | 50.17 | 415.5 | 26.30 | 689.7 | 48.81 | 1,949.1 | 64.17 | 3,451.0 | 50.79 |

## F. Resource-Based

| | | | | | | | | | | | |
|---|---|---|---|---|---|---|---|---|---|---|---|
| L-T Debt | 1,546.9 | 11.92 | 1,949.1 | 11.14 | 5,284.2 | 20.54 | 9,359.8 | 23.54 | 14,263.8 | 21.24 | 17,321.0 | 19.18 |
| Pf. Stock | 274.1 | 2.11 | 200.0 | 1.14 | 213.8 | 0.83 | 352.1 | 0.89 | 260.9 | 0.39 | 239.0 | 0.26 |
| Com. Stock | 2,930.0 | 22.57 | 4,552.0 | 26.01 | 4,941.7 | 19.21 | 4,701.5 | 11.82 | 7,057.1 | 10.51 | 7,904.4 | 8.75 |
| Ret. Earn. | 8,229.8 | 63.40 | 10,799.7 | 61.71 | 15,286.2 | 59.42 | 25,347.3 | 63.75 | 45,568.0 | 67.86 | 64,860.0 | 71.81 |

Source: Basic data were collected from Moody's Industrial Manual, 1960–1985 editions.

**Table 4.2**
**Composition of Capital Structure of the Control Firms, 1960–1984**

| Types of Capital | Years | | | | | | | | | | | |
|---|---|---|---|---|---|---|---|---|---|---|---|---|
| | 1960 | | 1965 | | 1970 | | 1975 | | 1980 | | 1984 | |
| | $Mill. | % | $Mill. | % | $Mill. | % | $Mill. | % | $Mill. | % | $Mill. | % |
| | | | | | A. High Technology | | | | | | | |
| L-T Debt | 874.5 | 21.76 | 2,084.2 | 32.97 | 4,542.9 | 31.46 | 6,577.0 | 31.46 | 7,730.6 | 24.33 | 10,507.3 | 24.22 |
| Pf. Stock | 84.2 | 2.09 | 219.7 | 3.47 | 669.7 | 4.64 | 799.4 | 3.85 | 1,617.2 | 5.09 | 1,510.1 | 3.50 |
| Com. Stock | 1,219.1 | 30.33 | 1,876.8 | 29.68 | 2,728.3 | 18.90 | 3,480.4 | 16.75 | 5,398.9 | 16.99 | 10,099.3 | 21.27 |
| Ret. Earn. | 1,842.1 | 45.82 | 2,142.3 | 33.88 | 6,492.6 | 45.00 | 9,923.9 | 47.75 | 17,026.1 | 53.59 | 21,267.3 | 49.01 |
| | | | | | B. Consumer Goods | | | | | | | |
| L-T Debt | 410.3 | 11.24 | 499.1 | 11.03 | 2,004.8 | 23.44 | 4,002.2 | 27.15 | 6,805.1 | 27.58 | 7,539.7 | 23.18 |
| Pf. Stock | 107.5 | 3.29 | 101.7 | 2.25 | 158.4 | 1.85 | 137.2 | 0.93 | 318.6 | 1.29 | 240.7 | 0.74 |
| Com. Stock | 880.1 | 26.97 | 1,303.9 | 28.81 | 1,842.1 | 21.54 | 2,426.2 | 16.47 | 2,638.4 | 10.69 | 3,438.8 | 10.58 |
| Ret. Earn. | 1,865.8 | 57.17 | 2,621.0 | 57.91 | 4,545.6 | 53.17 | 8,172.9 | 55.45 | 14,915.2 | 60.44 | 21,300.9 | 65.50 |
| | | | | | C. General Industrial | | | | | | | |
| L-T Debt | 417.1 | 11.24 | 746.7 | 10.59 | 1,593.5 | 16.61 | 2,395.7 | 18.71 | 6,546.5 | 24.86 | 7,413.8 | 25.17 |
| Pf. Stock | 14.3 | 0.38 | 17.5 | 0.25 | 19.3 | 0.20 | .4 | 0.56 | 623.4 | 2.37 | 55.7 | 0.19 |
| Com. Stock | 254.9 | 6.87 | 1,074.5 | 15.25 | 1,272.1 | 13.25 | 1,819.4 | 14.21 | 3,481.6 | 13.22 | 8,222.3 | 27.88 |
| Ret. Earn. | 3,026.2 | 81.51 | 5,208.7 | 73.91 | 6,713.9 | 69.94 | 8,515.3 | 66.52 | 15,684.9 | 59.55 | 13,802.9 | 46.80 |

## D. Service

| | | | | | | | | | | | |
|---|---|---|---|---|---|---|---|---|---|---|---|
| L-T Debt | 883.9 | 29.30 | 1,243.6 | 26.18 | 2,686.6 | 31.01 | 3,070.7 | 25.04 | 6,147.4 | 31.26 | 13,599.9 | 42.00 |
| Pf. Stock | ... | ... | 2.6 | 2.01 | 2.5 | 0.01 | 7.1 | 0.01 | 102.6 | 0.52 | 251.8 | 0.78 |
| Com. Stock | 441.2 | 13.73 | 660.1 | 13.90 | 909.3 | 10.49 | 1,703.5 | 13.88 | 1,783.3 | 9.07 | 2,233.1 | 6.90 |
| Ret. Earn. | 1,718.6 | 56.97 | 2,843.6 | 59.91 | 5,067.5 | 58.49 | 7,497.8 | 61.07 | 11,630.3 | 59.15 | 16,295.2 | 50.32 |

## E. Project Management

| | | | | | | | | | | | |
|---|---|---|---|---|---|---|---|---|---|---|---|
| L-T Debt | 87.5 | 27.93 | 93.3 | 21.76 | 366.0 | 42.54 | 482.3 | 43.28 | 399.5 | 24.09 | 583.9 | 26.18 |
| Pf. Stock | ... | ... | 16.0 | 3.73 | 5.1 | 0.59 | 1.9 | 0.17 | 50.1 | 3.03 | 160.1 | 7.15 |
| Com. Stock | 46.8 | 14.93 | 43.3 | 10.10 | 59.3 | 6.89 | 69.9 | 6.27 | 110.1 | 6.64 | 258.3 | 11.53 |
| Ret. Earn. | 176.2 | 57.14 | 276.1 | 64.41 | 430.1 | 49.98 | 560.3 | 50.28 | 1,098.4 | 66.24 | 1,237.2 | 55.24 |

## F. Resource-Based

| | | | | | | | | | | | |
|---|---|---|---|---|---|---|---|---|---|---|---|
| L-T Debt | 624.2 | 10.10 | 1,429.4 | 15.71 | 2,920.2 | 21.94 | 5,258.7 | 25.30 | 7,310.9 | 19.95 | 18,507.8 | 34.99 |
| Pf. Stock | ..... | ... | 10.7 | 0.12 | 10.9 | 0.01 | 11.6 | 0.01 | 563.3 | 1.54 | 1,007.1 | 1.90 |
| Com. Stock | 2,307.1 | 37.32 | 2,779.9 | 30.55 | 2,976.8 | 22.35 | 2,860.9 | 13.78 | 3,702.8 | 10.11 | 4,988.7 | 9.43 |
| Ret. Earn. | 3,250.3 | 52.58 | 4,878.5 | 53.62 | 7,425.0 | 55.70 | 12,659.6 | 61.91 | 25,055.5 | 68.40 | 28,384.6 | 53.68 |

**Table 4.3**
**Percentage Changes in the Capital Structure of the Excellent and Control Firms, 1960–1984**

| Industry Groupings | Years | | | | | |
|---|---|---|---|---|---|---|
| | 1960-1965 | 1965-1970 | 1970-1975 | 1975-1980 | 1980-1984 | 1960-1984 |
| A. Excellent Firms | | | | | | |
| High Tech. | 69.63 | 113.98 | 82.29 | 69.65 | 63.63 | 1,736.66 |
| Consumer Goods | 52.90 | 99.76 | 75.79 | 77.64 | 40.43 | 1,239.42 |
| General Indus. | 44.96 | 28.77 | 53.49 | 58.10 | 38.35 | 526.66 |
| Service | 32.21 | 142.14 | 99.70 | 87.46 | 69.56 | 1,932.04 |
| Project Manage. | 55.70 | 213.05 | -10.56 | 114.92 | 122.84 | 1,987.95 |
| Resource-Based | 34.82 | 46.99 | 54.56 | 68.88 | 34.51 | 595.83 |
| Total | 45.30 | 65.18 | 64.27 | 69.49 | 47.63 | 886.54 |
| B. Control Firms | | | | | | |
| High Tech. | 57.29 | 128.35 | 43.92 | 52.87 | 36.58 | 979.44 |
| Consumer Goods | 38.67 | 88.94 | 72.36 | 67.43 | 31.78 | 896.40 |
| General Indus. | 89.83 | 36.20 | 33.37 | 1,057.24 | 11.99 | 694.47 |
| Service | 57.45 | 82.45 | 41.69 | 60.14 | 64.67 | 973.36 |
| Project Manage. | 36.73 | 100.74 | 29.51 | 48.79 | 35.06 | 614.33 |
| Resource-Based | 47.19 | 46.54 | 55.94 | 76.20 | 44.37 | 755.58 |
| Total | 56.88 | 72.34 | 48.80 | 70.58 | 37.07 | 840.68 |

Source: Basic data were collected from Moody's Industrial Manual, 1960-1985 editions.

other three groupings in the same period. But it is interesting to note that even in 1984, retained earnings were over 50 percent in four groupings and slightly below that mark in the other two groupings. The picture was a bit brighter in 1960 when they were over 50 percent in five of the six industry groupings. As for the common stock, its percentage fell in five of the six groupings, while increasing only in general industrial during 1960–1984. This again shows less reliance on the issue of new common stocks in recent years due to the fear of dilution of ownership, the adverse effect on the price of the existing stocks, and of course, the absence of any tax advantage such as was prevalent on the issuance of bonds.

In table 4.3, we have shown the percentage changes in the aggregate capital of the six industry groupings during different subperiods and the twenty-five-year period for both the excellent and control firms. In the case of excellent firms, the highest rate of growth was in project management (but this sector consisted of only two firms), while the second-highest growth during the entire period took place in the service sector, followed by the high technology sector. Also, the highest growth in aggregate capital occurred during 1965–1970 (one of the longest sustained growth periods in the post–World War II U.S. economy) for both the high technology and the service sectors. Although project management registered the highest growth in capital during this period, it also showed the only negative growth during the next period. The data here, however, reflect the vagaries of an extremely small sample.

When we look into the aggregate growth of capital among the control firms, shown also in table 4.3, we find that the same trend was evident during the entire 1960–1984 period. Omitting the project management group, the highest growth in capital took place in high technology, followed by the service sector, and then by the consumer goods sector. But here also, the highest growth of capital among the five subperiods took place during 1965–1970 for high technology, consumer goods, the service sector, and of course, project management. The second-best period was 1975–1980, when the general industrial and resource-based sectors fared best both among the excellent and the control firms. Taken in the aggregate, the excellent firms showed only a slightly higher growth than the control firms during 1960–1984. Among the five subperiods, the highest aggregate growth of capital for the excellent firms took place during 1975–1980, followed by 1965–1970, while for the control firms the highest aggregate growth of capital occurred during 1965–1970, followed by 1975–1980. Obviously, (as far as our sample of firms was concerned), these two periods offered a more congenial environment for capital growth than the other periods.

In comparing the average annual compound growth rate among the four types of capital in the excellent and control groups, as shown in table 4.4, we find that overall, the growth rate was slightly higher among the excellent firms than the control firms during 1960–1984. For the excellent firms, the highest annual growth rate of capital took place in retained earnings, followed by long-term debt, with common stock taking third place. Retained earnings showed highest annual growth during 1970–1980, while the highest annual growth in long-term debt took place during 1960–1970. Interestingly, the highest growth of common stock took place during the more recent years of 1980–1984—years that also showed healthy growth in retained earnings and long-term debt. The negative showing of preferred

**Table 4.4**
**Average Annual Compound Growth Rates of Capital of the Excellent and Control Firms, 1960–1984**

| Types of Capital | Years | | | |
|---|---|---|---|---|
| | 1960-1970 | 1970-1980 | 1980-1984 | 1960-1984 |
| **A. Excellent Firms** | | | | |
| Long-term Debt | 11.96 | 9.63 | 10.17 | 10.69 |
| Preferred Stock | -1.45 | 15.69 | -2.50 | 5.17 |
| Common Stock | 7.19 | 5.49 | 9.39 | 6.84 |
| Retained Earnings | 9.20 | 12.29 | 10.58 | 10.71 |
| Total | 9.15 | 10.78 | 10.23 | 10.01 |
| **B. Control Firms** | | | | |
| Long-term Debt | 15.65 | 9.49 | 13.58 | 12.70 |
| Preferred stock | 10.64 | 14.23 | -0.31 | 12.16 |
| Common Stock | 6.69 | 5.75 | 14.33 | 7.53 |
| Retained Earnings | 9.95 | 10.78 | 14.33 | 7.53 |
| Total | 10.46 | 9.76 | 8.20 | 9.79 |

Source: Basic data were collected from Moody's Industrial Manual,
        1960-1985 editions.

stock only indicated the fact that many of them were retired as the years went on.

For the control firms, in 1960–1984 the highest annual growth rate was registered by long-term debt, followed by preferred stock, and then by retained earnings. Also, as was seen in the case of excellent firms, the highest annual growth of long-term debt took place during 1960–1970, while for the retained earnings such growth took place during 1970–1980. The trend was similar for common stock, which grew at the maximum rate during the more recent period, 1980–1984. Again, the negative sign of preferred stock meant more stocks of this kind were recalled and retired during 1980–1984 than at any time before, which was true for both kinds of stocks. It is interesting to note that capital growth was quite high for both the excellent and control firms during 1980–1984, when, in many other respects, the financial health of these firms deteriorated considerably, as was seen in the earlier analysis.

## TESTING OF OPTIMAL CAPITAL STRUCTURE

Following the model of Richard Castanias, we may test the optimal capital structure of a firm or group of firms by examining the trend of key capital structure ratios (i.e., whether they are increasing or decreasing over time).[7] Here we have selected six financial ratios to test the optimal of capital structure for our sample of firms:

1. Long-term debt to total assets (LTD/TA)
2. Long-term debt to net worth (LTD/NW)
3. Long-term debt to total capital (LTD/TC)
4. Total liabilities to net worth (TL/NW)
5. Net worth to total assets (NW/TA)
6. Cash flow to long-term debt (CF/LTD)

Table 4.5 indicates the direction of signs for the optimal capital structure as incorporated in these financial ratios.

Following the optimal capital structure hypothesis, we would expect the ratio of long-term debt to total assets to decrease over time as the risk of bankruptcy becomes more and more important. Similarly, in an optimum capital structure, the ratio of long-term debt to net worth would decrease over time, as would the ratio of long-term debt to total capital, and long-term debt to net worth. Since the assets of a successful company should generate more and more net worth, we would expect the ratio of net worth to total assets to increase over time. Finally, a successful company should also generate higher cash flow so that the ratio of cash flow to long-term debt would also increase over time.

In table 4.6, we calculated the ratio of long-term debt to total assets and the ratio of long-term debt to net worth for both the excellent and control firms during 1975–1984. With respect to the ratio of long-term debt to total assets, the excellent firms did somewhat better than the control firms. The ratio went down in four out of six industry groupings among the excellent firms, as our theory of optimal capital structure suggests should occur, while for the control firms, the ratio went down clearly in three out of the six groupings from 1975–1984. Among the excellent firms, the ratio went up in project management, while remaining virtually constant in the consumer goods sector. Among the control firms, however, it went up only slightly in the general industrial sector, while remaining almost constant in the service and resource-based sectors. But when we compare the change in ratio from 1980 to 1984, we find that it went up in four

**Table 4.5**
**Financial Ratios and the Signs of Optimal Capital Structure**

| Financial Ratios | Signs of Optimal Capital Structure |
|---|---|
| LTD/TA | Decreasing over Time |
| LTD/NW | Decreasing over Time |
| LTD/TC | Decreasing over Time |
| TL/NW | Decreasing over Time |
| NW/TA | Increasing over Time |
| CF/LTD | Increasing over Time |

of the six industry groupings in both the excellent and control firms, indicating that although the overall trend was toward optimal capital structure, the situation had deteriorated for both groups during the later part of our study.

When we examine the ratio of long-term debt to net worth we find the situation to be slightly reversed between the two groups, as the control firms did slightly better than the excellent firms, on average. When compared with 1975, the ratio in 1984 fell in four out of the six industry groupings among the control firms, while it fell in only three groupings among the excellent firms during the same period. Also, it went up in three groupings among the control firms during 1980–1984, but in four industry groupings among the excellent firms during the same period. Interestingly, for both the control firms and the excellent firms this ratio was lowest in the consumer goods sector both in 1975 and 1984. It was, however, highest in the service sector among the excellent firms in both 1975 and 1984, whereas among the control firms, it was highest in project management in 1975 and in the resource-based sector in 1984.

When we compare the ratio of long-term debt to total capital for the excellent firms with the same ratio for the control firms, as shown in table 4.7, we find that the excellent firms as a whole did relatively better than the control firms. Among the excellent firms the ratio fell in five of the six industry groupings from 1975 to 1984, while increasing slightly in the service sector. Among the control firms, the ratio fell in four of the six groupings, although here, too, it increased slightly in the remaining two groupings. From 1980 to 1984, however, the ratio went up in four of the six groupings among the excellent firms, while increasing slightly in only three of the six groupings among the control firms. This indicates that this aspect of capital structure had deteriorated more for the excellent firms than the control firms in the later part of our study.

**Table 4.6**

**Ratios of Long-term Debt to Total Assets, and Long-term Debt to Net Worth of the Excellent and Control Firms, 1975–1984**

| Industry Groupings | Long-term Debt/Total Assets | | | Long-term Debt/Net Worth | | |
|---|---|---|---|---|---|---|
| | 1975 | 1980 | 1984 | 1975 | 1980 | 1984 |
| A. Excellent Firms | | | | | | |
| High Tech. | 0.2152 | 0.1379 | 0.0913 | 0.3997 | 0.4853 | 0.1978 |
| Consumer Goods | 0.1269 | 0.0944 | 0.1245 | 0.2217 | 0.1790 | 0.1964 |
| General Indus. | 0.2162 | 0.1603 | 0.1833 | 0.4520 | 0.3890 | 0.4625 |
| Service | 0.2404 | 0.1827 | 0.2119 | 0.6231 | 0.3746 | 0.6448 |
| Project Manage. | 0.0105 | 0.0360 | 0.1905 | 0.280 | 0.1045 | 0.2715 |
| Resource-Based | 0.1818 | 0.1510 | 0.1434 | 0.4527 | 0.3674 | 0.3550 |
| B. Control Firms | | | | | | |
| High Tech. | 0.2211 | 0.1582 | 0.1876 | 0.5228 | 0.3573 | 0.4412 |
| Consumer Goods | 0.2919 | 0.1803 | 0.1828 | 0.3501 | 0.3511 | 0.3198 |
| General Indus. | 0.1932 | 0.1739 | 0.2032 | 0.3394 | 0.2139 | 0.4097 |
| Service | 0.1812 | 0.1774 | 0.1859 | 0.6791 | 0.5204 | 0.5525 |
| Project Manage. | 0.3210 | 0.1677 | 0.1619 | 0.0100 | 0.5245 | 0.3830 |
| Resource-Based | 0.2483 | 0.1825 | 0.2499 | 0.5629 | 0.4028 | 0.6347 |

Source: Basic data were collected from Moody's Industrial Manual, 1960-1985 editions.

Table 4.7 also shows the ratio of total liabilities to net worth for the two groupings during 1975–1984. This provides a broad measure of leverage in the total capital structure. Overall, the trend among the excellent firms was only a little better than among the control firms, since the ratio fell in four of the six groupings among the excellent firms during 1975–1984, while it went down clearly in only two of the six groupings among the control firms. (It remained virtually constant in two groupings among the control firms during the same period.) During 1980–1984, the ratio went up in three industry groupings among the excellent firms, but it increased in only one grouping among the control firms. Again, among the excellent firms, the ratio was lowest in the consumer goods sector both in 1975 and 1984, while it was second also among the control firms in 1975, and lowest in 1984—a trend for the consumer goods sector we noticed before in the ratio of long-term debt to total capital. Clearly, among both groups, firms in the consumer goods sector were on average closer to

**Table 4.7**

**Ratios of Long-term Debt to Total Capital, and Total Liabilities to Net Worth of the Excellent and Control Firms, 1975–1984**

| Industry Groupings | Long-term Debt/ Total Capital | | | Total Liabilities/ Net Worth | | |
|---|---|---|---|---|---|---|
| | 1975 | 1980 | 1984 | 1975 | 1980 | 1984 |
| A. Excellent Firms | | | | | | |
| High Tech. | 0.2816 | 0.2434 | 0.1512 | 1.1382 | 0.9646 | 0.8895 |
| Consumer Goods | 0.1697 | 0.1280 | 0.1479 | 0.5632 | 0.6614 | 0.4841 |
| General Indus. | 0.3032 | 0.2525 | 0.2862 | 0.9695 | 1.0542 | 1.0857 |
| Service | 0.3411 | 0.2508 | 0.3514 | 1.0728 | 1.2866 | 1.3570 |
| Project Manage. | 0.2500 | 0.0830 | 0.1500 | 1.3085 | 0.7895 | 0.9945 |
| Resource-Based | 0.2915 | 0.2584 | 0.2457 | 1.0467 | 1.0055 | 0.9241 |
| B. Control Firms | | | | | | |
| High Tech. | 0.2754 | 0.2272 | 0.2690 | 1.1889 | 1.2782 | 1.1712 |
| Consumer Goods | 0.2966 | 0.2478 | 0.2359 | 0.8441 | 0.9087 | 0.8429 |
| General Indus. | 0.2730 | 0.2482 | 0.2845 | 0.7706 | 0.8413 | 1.0543 |
| Service | 0.2900 | 0.3029 | 0.2868 | 1.5867 | 1.4950 | 1.4661 |
| Project Manage. | 0.4676 | 0.2862 | 0.2685 | 1.7400 | 1.1600 | 1.1650 |
| Resource-Based | 0.3291 | 0.2503 | 0.3541 | 1.2841 | 1.5609 | 1.4543 |

Source: Basic data were collected from Moody's Industrial Manual, 1960–1985 editions.

optimum capital structure than those in any other sector during the period covered by our study.

In table 4.8, we have calculated the ratio of net worth to total assets as well as the ratio of cash flow to long-term debt for both the excellent and the control firms. According to the optimal capital structure theory, both ratios should increase over time in a healthy firm or sector. For the excellent firms and the control firms, the ratio of net worth to total assets did go up in four out of the six industry groupings from 1975 to 1984. Among the excellent firms, in 1984 the ratio was highest in the consumer goods sector, followed by high technology, and then by project management, but it went down most sharply in the service sector, and only slightly in the general industrial sector. Among the control firms, however, the highest increase of the ratio from 1975 to 1984 was witnessed in the service sector, followed by high technology, while the ratio declined modestly

**Table 4.8**
**Ratio of Net Worth to Total Assets, and Cash Flow to Long-term Debt of the Excellent and Control Firms, 1975–1984**

| Industry Groupings | Net Worth/ Total Assets | | | Cash Flow/ Long-term Debt | | |
|---|---|---|---|---|---|---|
| | 1975 | 1980 | 1984 | 1975 | 1980 | 1984 |
| A. Excellent Firms | | | | | | |
| High Tech. | 0.4654 | 0.4608 | 0.5385 | 2.4716 | 2.1608 | 2.6012 |
| Consumer Goods | 0.6172 | 0.5770 | 0.6614 | 2.3747 | 2.6905 | 2.1800 |
| General Indus. | 0.5610 | 0.5283 | 0.5498 | 0.7972 | 1.0263 | 1.2482 |
| Service | 0.4611 | 0.4406 | 0.3469 | 2.7986 | 2.4110 | 1.5917 |
| Project Manage. | 0.3205 | 0.3950 | 0.4800 | 11.6800 | 3.5250 | 3.4055 |
| Resource-Based | 0.4395 | 0.4191 | 0.4439 | 1.7868 | 2.4974 | 1.7961 |
| B. Control Firms | | | | | | |
| High Tech. | 0.6673 | 0.6015 | 0.7897 | 0.8073 | 2.5360 | 2.1578 |
| Consumer Goods | 0.5193 | 0.5431 | 0.6234 | 3.5005 | 1.4259 | 1.0475 |
| General Indus. | 0.5714 | 0.5854 | 0.5023 | 1.1163 | 1.5637 | 1.1638 |
| Service | 0.3109 | 0.4620 | 0.4930 | 0.7265 | 0.7556 | 1.7477 |
| Project Manage. | 0.3379 | 0.3702 | 0.4029 | 0.3041 | 1.0355 | -.2080 |
| Resource-Based | 0.4355 | 0.4351 | 0.3910 | 0.5769 | 1.2573 | 0.6915 |

Source: Basic data were collected from Moody's Industrial Manual, 1960–1985 editions.

both in general industrial and the resource-based sectors. Also, the level of this ratio was much higher among the control firms than among the excellent firms. On average, the ratio of net worth to total capital increased by 12.66 percent for the control firms during 1975–1984, but for the excellent firms it increased by only 5.45 percent during the same period.

When we examine the ratio of cash flow to long-term debt for both groups during 1975–1984, we find that for the excellent firms, the ratio grew in the high technology and general industrial sectors, but fell in the consumer goods, service, and project management sectors while remaining virtually unchanged in the resource-based sector. But among the control firms, the ratio increased more clearly in three of the six industry groupings and fell in only two groupings while remaining the same in the general industrial sector. The ratio deteriorated in most sectors for both groups of firms during 1980–1984 as compared to 1975–1980, but the decline was more pronounced for the excellent firms than the control firms. On average, the ratio of cash flow to long-term debt declined by 14 percent during 1975–1984 for the excellent firms, whereas for the control firms, this ratio fell by only 0.22 percent during the same period.

Another approach to judging the optimal capital structure of a firm is to focus on the relationship between the earnings per share of the firm and its debt-asset ratio (i.e., its total debt, including current liabilities, divided by total assets). The underlying theory behind this approach is that in a risk-return world of reality, the higher the financial leverage of a firm, the higher its earnings per share will be, and vice versa. With increased financial leverage, as measured using the debt ratio, we would expect a corresponding decline in the firm's ability to make scheduled interest payments, as measured using the times-interest-earned (TIE) ratio. This would increase default and other risks. To offset these risks, the return must be higher. Thus we would expect a positive correlation between the debt-asset ratio and the attendant earnings per share.

In table 4.9 we have calculated the total debt/asset ratio and the earnings per share of the thirty-one excellent firms on Peters and Waterman's list, which passed all their tests of excellence. We have examined the debt-asset ratio and the earnings per share (EPS) for two periods, 1975 and 1984. Here we find that in the majority of cases, the relationship between these two variables was not positive, as the optimal capital structure theory would dictate it should be. Here the increasing debt-asset ratio was not accompanied by increasing earnings per share during 1975–1984. In sixteen out of thirty-one firms, the debt-asset ratio went down when the earnings per share of the firm in question went up, or vice versa. In thirteen cases, the EPS went up when the debt-asset ratio also went up. And, in two cases, the EPS went down when the debt-asset ratio also went down.

Even when the two variables moved in the same direction the magnitudes were quite random in nature. Following the capital structure theory we would expect that return must be commensurate with risk (i.e., there should be a close correspondence between the percentage change in the debt-asset ratio and earnings per share). But in those cases when both variables showed increment, we find that a less than 5 percent increase in debt-asset ratio was accompanied by a 256 percent increase in the earnings per share, as in the case of Delta Airlines, or an 11 percent decrease in debt-asset ratio was followed by a 98 percent decrease in earnings per share, as in the case of Fluor during 1975–1984. Similarly, a 229 percent increase in debt-asset ratio for Disney Productions was associated with only a 50 percent increase in earnings per share during the same time period. Evidently,

**Table 4.9**
**Debt/Asset Ratio and the Earnings per Share of the 31 Excellent Firms, 1975–1984**

| Name of the Excellent Firm | Debt/Asset Ratio | | | Earnings per Share | | |
|---|---|---|---|---|---|---|
| | 1975 | 1984 | % Change | 1975 | 1984 | % Change |
| Avon | 33.96 | 44.47 | +30.95 | 2.90 | 2.16 | -25.52 |
| Boeing | 40.84 | 50.96 | +24.78 | 0.53 | 2.67 | +403.77 |
| Bristol-Myers | 38.07 | 29.71 | -21.96 | 0.56 | 1.73 | +208.93 |
| Caterpillar | 48.01 | 53.39 | +11.21 | 4.65 | (2.60) | -155.91 |
| Dana Corp. | 42.03 | 38.78 | -7.73 | 1.42 | 3.52 | +147.89 |
| Data General | 23.08 | 43.38 | +87.95 | 0.76 | 2.60 | +242.11 |
| Delta Airlines | 44.89 | 46.93 | +4.54 | 1.24 | 4.42 | +256.45 |
| Digital Equipment | 29.05 | 27.21 | -6.33 | (1.57) | 0.64 | +140.76 |
| Disney Productions | 10.24 | 40.22 | +292.77 | 0.48 | 0.75 | +56.25 |
| Dow Chemical | 52.13 | 47.35 | -9.17 | 3.33 | 2.50 | -24.92 |
| Du Pont | 34.04 | 35.68 | +4.82 | 1.81 | 5.89 | +225.41 |
| Eastman Kodak | 23.89 | 27.07 | +13.31 | 1.69 | 2.54 | +50.30 |
| Fluor | 50.76 | 44.74 | -11.86 | 0.95 | 0.01 | -98.94 |
| Hewlett-Packard | 23.99 | 27.23 | +13.51 | 0.38 | 2.13 | +460.53 |
| Intel | 20.88 | 26.98 | +29.21 | 0.14 | 1.02 | +628.57 |
| I.B.M. | 23.55 | 30.15 | +28.03 | 3.34 | 10.77 | +222.46 |
| Johnson & Johnson | 22.92 | 27.90 | +21.73 | 1.06 | 2.75 | +159.43 |
| K-Mart | 43.48 | 39.49 | -9.18 | 1.09 | 2.56 | +134.86 |
| Marriott | 56.32 | 58.16 | +3.27 | 0.13 | 1.00 | +669.23 |
| Maytag | 25.57 | 28.21 | +10.32 | 0.49 | 1.16 | +136.73 |
| Mc Donald's | 54.19 | 24.71 | -54.40 | 0.43 | 1.95 | +353.49 |
| Merck | 48.14 | 31.18 | -35.23 | -.51 | 1.12 | +119.61 |
| Minnesota Mining | 34.61 | 29.17 | +157.18 | 1.15 | 3.14 | +173.04 |
| National Semiconductor | 39.11 | 37.06 | -5.53 | 0.30 | 0.66 | +1.20 |
| Procter & Gamble | 35.90 | 35.78 | -0.33 | 2.03 | 5.17 | +154.68 |
| Raychem | 52.43 | 35.91 | -315.09 | 0.49 | 1.02 | +108.16 |
| Schlumberger | 36.35 | 34.29 | -5.67 | 0.77 | 4.10 | +432.47 |
| Standard Oil (Ind.) /Amoco | 38.88 | 32.72 | -15.84 | 2.68 | 7.51 | +180.22 |
| Texas Instruments | 37.11 | 52.37 | +41.12 | 0.90 | 4.24 | +371.11 |
| Wal-Mart | 49.61 | 32.90 | -33.68 | 0.03 | 0.48 | +1,500.00 |
| Wang Laboratories | 48.96 | 39.99 | -18.32 | 0.04 | 1.51 | +3,675.00 |

Source: Basic data were collected from Moody's Industrial Manuals, various issues covering 1975-1984.

capital structure was not optimal for the overwhelming number of these so-called excellent firms as far as the correlation between debt-asset ratio and the accompanying earnings per share were concerned.

## STOCK VALUATION ANALYSIS OF
## THE EXCELLENT FIRMS

The main problems for future stock valuations are that the amount and timing of future dividends are not fully known, the amount and growth of future earnings are not known with certainty, and the price of stocks at the time they will be sold is uncertain. Thus, to undertake the stock valuation process, we have to make certain simplified assumptions that should not veer too much from the real world situation. Our main objective here is to determine whether the market price of the stock involved is overvalued, undervalued, or fairly valued in relation to its "true" or intrinsic value. For the purpose of long-term investment, we are obviously interested in those stocks that are relatively undervalued at the time of investment, following the simple "buy and hold" trading rule.

The most popular stock valuation model is the Gordon Model, which assumes that the price of stock is the present value of the stream of future dividends.[8] Even if a company does not pay much dividend, the valuation model will incorporate the growth of dividends and will presume that any capital gain will be reflected in the future price of the stock. For our analysis, we will assume that the dividend is growing at the constant rate as computed from the past trend, and the earnings rate is also growing at the constant rate calculated from the historical data. The holding period of the stock is three years, which has been found to be generally true for the average stock listed on the New York Stock Exchange.[9]

The basic valuation model is as follows:

$$V_0 = \sum_{t=1}^{n} \frac{D_t}{(1 + k)^t} + \frac{P_n}{(1 + k)^n} \tag{1}$$

where $V_0$ is the present value of the stock; $D_t$ is the dividend at the period $t$; $P_n$ is the price prevailing at the holding period $n$; and $k$ is the discount or risk-capitalization rate as determined by the judgment of the investor.

For the growth stock, the basic valuation model becomes:

$$V_0 = \frac{D_0(1 + g_d)^1}{(1 + k)^1} + \frac{D_0(1 + g_d)^2}{(1 + k)^2} + \frac{D_0(1 + g_d)^3 + P_3}{(1 + k)^3} \tag{2}$$

where $V_0$ is the present value of the stock; $D_0$ is the dividend in year 0; $g_d$ is the annual growth rate of dividends; and $P_3$ is the price expected in year 3, which is some function of $E_3$ (earnings per share in year 3) times the price-earnings ratio in year 3 $(P/E)_3$, based on the growth of earnings in years 4, 5, 6 . . . $n$. The equation for $P_3$ may be written as $P_3 = E_0 (1 + g_e)^3 (P/E)_3$, where $E_0$ is the earnings per share in year 0; $g_e$ is the expected growth rate of earnings per share; and $(P/E)_3$ is the price-earnings ratio expected in year 3. Then the complete model becomes:

$$V_0 = \sum_{t=1}^{3} \frac{D_0(1 + g_d)^t}{(1 + k)^t} + \frac{E_0(1 + g_e)^3(P/E)_3}{(1 + k)^3} \qquad (3)$$

For our calculation, we have taken the ten-year average growth rates of dividends and earnings per share of the companies during 1975–1984. For the price-earnings ratio, Amling mentioned a normal $P/E$ ratio for the Standard & Poor 500 stock index to be 11.1.[10] We have taken that figure for the estimation of the expected price of a stock in period 3 $(P_3)$. The thorniest problem is to select the capitalization or discount rate for the stock valuation. Fisher and Lorie found that the common stock returned 9 percent per year for the period 1926–1960, which may be taken as an average risk-capitalization rate for the valuation process.[11] We have taken that figure as our discount rate for the calculation.

Table 4.10 shows the intrinsic value as well as the average market value of stocks of almost all the excellent firms prevailing in 1984. The result was exactly even, as the intrinsic value of twenty-three stocks was higher than their respective market value, whereas the market value of twenty-three stocks was higher than the intrinsic value, as of 1984. Thus the number of stocks undervalued was the same as the number of stocks overvalued, equaling the "buy" or "sell" recommendations. But we would normally expect the stocks of the excellent firms to be good buys, having higher intrinsic values than their market values. That did not happen in the majority of cases. We should remember, however, that the limitations of assumptions of the constant-growth dividend valuation model as used here would affect all the excellent firms almost equally during the period covered. That analysis proves that even by using the fundamental analysis of stock valuation, the stockholders of the excellent firms would come out even as a group, giving them no additional advantage to aid in outperforming the other stocks, or the stock market as a whole.

**Table 4.10**
**Stock Market Valuation of the Excellent Firms**

| Name of the Company | Intrinsic Value of the Stock | Average Market Price of the Stock, 1984 | Decision Rule |
|---|---|---|---|
| High Technology | | | |
| Amdahl | $11.42 | $14.87 | Sell |
| Digital Equipment | 28.26 | 90.81 | Sell |
| Emerson Electric | 71.45 | 32.72 | Buy |
| Gould | 6.99 | 27.75 | Sell |
| Hewlett-Packard | 89.48 | 41.31 | Buy |
| NCR | 63.38 | 26.81 | Buy |
| Rockwell | 25.02 | 28.31 | Sell |
| United Technologies | 43.40 | 35.06 | Buy |
| Westinghouse | 22.90 | 24.06 | Sell |
| Xerox | 43.75 | 48.87 | Sell |
| General Electric | 64.45 | 53.81 | Buy |
| Intel | 6.43 | 31.81 | Sell |
| Lockheed | 47.33 | 39.44 | Buy |
| National Semiconductor | 9.12 | 14.12 | Sell |
| Raychem | 68.47 | 65.31 | Buy |
| TRW | 85.43 | 70.37 | Buy |
| Wang Laboratories | NMF | ... | ... |
| Consumer Goods | | | |
| Blue Bell | $39.36 | $30.94 | Buy |
| Eastman Kodak | 85.30 | 106.00 | Sell |
| General Foods | 51.46 | 52.50 | Sell |
| Johnson & Johnson | 39.67 | 83.50 | Sell |
| Procter & Gamble | 62.32 | 72.75 | Sell |
| Avon | 24.91 | 35.91 | Sell |
| Bristol Myers | 37.88 | 46.82 | Sell |
| Chesebrough-Pond's | 39.28 | 35.98 | Buy |
| Levi Strauss | 17.70 | 33.06 | Sell |
| Maytag | 70.76 | 45.62 | Buy |
| Merck | 149.33 | 87.87 | Buy |
| Polaroid | 29.66 | 30.06 | Sell |
| Revlon | 36.93 | 44.80 | Sell |

**Table 4.10**  (continued)

| Name of the Company | Intrinsic Value of the Stock | Average Market Price of the Stock, 1984 | Decision Rule |
|---|---|---|---|
| General Industrial | | | |
| Caterpillar Tractor | NMF | ... | ... |
| Dana Corporation | 63.65 | 26.12 | Buy |
| Ingersoll-Rand | 33.63 | 45.62 | Sell |
| McDermott | NMF | ... | ... |
| Minnesota Mining | 158.63 | 77.37 | Buy |
| Service | | | |
| Delta Airlines | 38.04 | 45.56 | Sell |
| Marriott | 92.48 | 69.37 | Buy |
| McDonald's | 91.93 | 64.67 | Buy |
| American Airlines | 43.67 | 9.05 | Buy |
| Disney Productions | 62.92 | 56.87 | Buy |
| K-Mart | 56.34 | 32.19 | Buy |
| Wal-Mart | 28.90 | 38.62 | Sell |
| Project Management | | | |
| Boeing | 44.39 | 47.56 | Sell |
| Fluor | NMF | ... | ... |
| Resource-Based | | | |
| Arco | 59.05 | 46.56 | Buy |
| Dow Chemical | 27.68 | 30.00 | Sell |
| Du Pont | 54.56 | 47.67 | Buy |
| Standard Oil Ind./Amoco | 89.15 | 54.38 | Buy |

NMF = Not meaningful due to losses in the initial terminal year of this study.

## NOTES

1. M. Bradley, G. Jarrell, and E. Kim, "On the Existence of an Optimal Capital Structure: Theory and Evidence," *Journal of Finance*, Vol. 39 (July 1984):857–78.

2. F. Modigliani and M. Miller, "The Cost of Capital, Corporation Finance and the Theory of Investments," *American Economic Review*, Vol. 48 (June 1958):261–97.

3. M. Miller, "Debt and taxes," *Journal of Finance*, Vol. 32 (1977):261–75.

4. H. DeAngello and R. Masulis, "Optimal Capital Structure under Corporate and Personal Taxation," *Journal of Financial Economics*, Vol. 8 (March 1980):3–29.

5. F. Amling, *Investments* (Englewood Cliffs, N.J.: Prentice-Hall, 1984), p. 424.

6. M. Brealey and S. Myers, *Principles of Corporate Finance* (New York: McGraw-Hill, 1981), p. 374.

7. Richard Castanias, "Bankruptcy Risk and Optimal Capital Structure," *Journal of Finance*, Vol. 38 (Dec. 1983):1617–35.

8. For a brief description of the Gordon Model, see Amling, *Investments*, pp. 457–66.

9. New York Stock Exchange *Fact Book*, published by The New York Stock Exchange, 1982 edition.

10. Frederick Amling, *Investments* 461.

11. L. Fisher and J. Lorie, "Rates of Return on Investments in Common Stock," *Journal of Business*, Vol. 43 (April 1970), pp. 99–134.

# 5

# Corporate Acquisitions and Stockholders' Wealth in the United States' Excellent Firms

While Peters and Waterman, in their book *In Search of Excellence*, mainly undertook their analyses of firm excellence from the management's point of view, the question remains as to whether the shareholders of these companies also reaped above-average returns, as compared to the not-so-excellent control group of firms, during the period covered by their study (1960–1982). Since the stockholders are the real owners of public companies, the nature and magnitude of the returns they receive should be the paramount factor in judging the firms for their excellence in performance. In this chapter we want to examine whether the stockholders of these excellent companies earned any abnormally positive or excess returns when they acquired other firms during 1960–1984.

## TESTING OF THE HYPOTHESIS AND "EVENT STUDIES" METHODOLOGY

There is a great deal of controversy in finance as to the nature of abnormal returns earned by the acquiring firms, although the overwhelming majority of studies have found that the shareholders of the acquired firms do earn positive abnormal returns on the eve of acquisitions. Mandelker was one of the first researchers who explicitly used the Capital Asset Pricing Model (CAPM) in determining residuals (i.e., abnormal returns).[1] He found that stockholders of the acquiring firms earned normal returns during the pre- and post-merger periods, while stockholders of the acquired firms earned significant abnormal returns in the seven months preceding the completion of mergers. Franks, Broyles, and Hecht also found later that the consolidated firms earned a normal rate of return.[2] But Ellert, using the same methodology and a much longer sample for an overlapping period, found that stockholders of the acquiring firms earned significant positive abnormal returns over the seven months before the effective date of merger.[3] Similarly, Dodd and Ruback, taking the tender offers (date of public announcement of the merger) rather than the completion date of the merger, found that the largest firms earned significant abnormal returns in the month in which the offer was announced, regardless of whether it was accepted or not.[4] They reported that stockholders of successful bidding firms earned a small abnormal return in the month of announcement. Halpern, however, found that the acquiring firms as well as the acquired firms earned positive abnormal returns.[5]

When compared with the non-merging control group of firms, the results were also mixed. Reid[6] and Hogarty[7] reported inferior post-merger price performance with respect to a non-merging control group, while Shick and Jen found superior performance.[8] Langetieg compared the performance of merging firms to a control group of firms in the same industry that did not merge.[9] He found the abnormal returns to the acquiring firms not to be significantly positive. The widely quoted study by Paul Asquith had also supported the findings of Mandelker, Langetieg, and Dodd— that the acquired firms' stockholders earn large positive abnormal returns from the merger, and the acquiring firms' stockholders are affected little, if at all.[10]

The hypothesis we would like to test in this study is: Did the excellent firms earn higher positive abnormal returns for their stockholders than the non-excellent firms (our control firms) in their acquisitions during the period covered by Peters and Waterman's study and brought up-to-date? We would generally expect that, because of their better selection process for acquiring firms, superior negotiating skills, supposedly better management, large-scale extension of product-lines, and the reduction of business risks, the excellent firms would earn higher positive abnormal returns from mergers as compared to the non-excellent firms. If, on the other hand, the control firms earned higher positive abnormal returns than the excellent firms from mergers, then they, in fact, have become excellent in terms of providing higher returns to their stockholders than the so-called excellent firms listed by Peters and Waterman.

The research methodology we follow is that of "event" studies. Since the path-breaking article published by Fama, Fisher, Jensen, and Roll, concerning their study of the announcement of stock splits, event study methodology has been used extensively for calculating the impact on stock prices and stock returns of new market issues, exchange listings, announcements of accounting changes, annual and quarterly earnings reports, depreciation and inventory changes, and of course, mergers and acquisitions, among other factors.[11] The basic assumption of the event study methodology is the Efficient Market Hypothesis (EMH) of the semistrong form, which asserts that security prices adjust rapidly to the release of *all new public information.* (The weak form assumes the current stock prices fully reflect *all stock market information,* while the strong form contends that stock prices fully reflect *all information,* public or otherwise.)

There are generally two ways of calculating average abnormal returns (AAR)—the "market" model and the "comparison period" model. The unique relationship between a stock and the market returns for a period prior to and subsequent to a significant economic event can be calculated with the help of Standard & Poor's market index of 500 common stocks. There are quite a few varieties of market models, a good description of which can be found in Brown and Warner.[12]

The comparison period approach was used very successfully by Brown and Warner to compute abnormal returns. This study has shown that the comparison period approach works as well as the more sophisticated market model in detecting abnormal performance when it is present. To determine the monthly abnormal returns of a security, we first calculate the average monthly return over a specified interval—the comparison period. This comparison period return (CPR) is taken as an estimate of the expected monthly return for the period under study—the "observation period." The CPR for our comparison period calculation was based on the average monthly returns from month $-48$ through month $-13$, totalling thirty-six months. The observation period extends from month $-12$ through month $+12$.

We have used both the comparison period model and the market model for the calculation of abnormal returns. However, we would like to report the results of the market model here. The market model we used is the *Risk (beta)-Adjusted Market Model,* where the unique relationship between a stock and the market can be derived by computing a regression of stock returns and the market returns (i.e., the beta coefficient) prior to and subsequent to a significant economic event as follows:

$$R_{jt} = a_j + B_j R_{mt} + e \qquad (1)$$

where:

$R_{jt}$ = the rate of return on security $j$ during period $t$,

$a_j$ = the intercept or constant for security $j$ in the regression,

$B_j$ = the regression slope coefficient for security $j$ equal to $cov_{jm}/\sigma_m^2$,

$R_{mt}$ = the rate of return on a market index during period $t$,

$e$ = a random error term that sums to zero.

After calculating the expected return $E(R_{jt})$ from the above equation, the abnormal return $(AR_{jt})$ would be equal to the *actual* return minus the *expected* return:

$$AR_{jt} = R_{jt} - E(R_{jt}) \tag{2}$$

We have taken sixty months prior to the observation period for the calculation of the beta-coefficient $(B_j)$ for each security. The average abnormal return (AAR) is obtained for each month over the 25-month observation period by using the formula:

$$AAR_n = \frac{\sum_{j=1}^{n} a_{jm}}{n} \tag{3}$$

where: $n$ = number of sample securities, $a_{jm}$ = abnormal return for security $j$ on month $m$, $AAR_m$ = average abnormal return for month $m$.

The cumulative average abnormal return (CAAR) for month $m$ is defined by:

$$CAAR_m = \sum_{k=-12}^{m} AAR_k \tag{4}$$

A $t$-statistic that tests whether the average abnormal return for month $m$ is significantly different than zero is calculated, following Jain,[13] by:

$$t_m = AAR_m/s \tag{5}$$

where $s$ is the estimated standard deviation of the $AAR_s$ calculated from the comparison period (month $-48$ to month $-13$) relative to the event month for each firm. Similarly, the $t$-statistic of CAAR for a period of $N$ months from month $a$ to month $b$ is calculated by:

$$t_{ab} = \text{CAAR}_{ab}/s\sqrt{N} \tag{6}$$

For our study, we have examined the acquisition of other firms by those firms that were termed excellent by Peters and Waterman in their book *In Search of Excellence*. Out of a list of sixty-two U.S. firms, fifty-six were public companies, and fifty-three belonged to the New York Stock Exchange. We have examined those firms that belonged to NYSE, and then the acquisitions by those excellent firms that met the following criteria:

1. The acquiring firms were engaged in a successful merger or acquisition between January 1, 1960, and December 31, 1984, in which the book value of the assets of the acquired firm was greater than 10 percent of the book value of assets of the acquiring firm;

2. The acquiring firm had no other merger for one year preceding and one year after the acquisition of the firm in question;

3. The acquiring firm was listed in the New York Stock Exchange at least six years before and one year after the merger was announced.

Only twenty-nine excellent firms met these requirements. For our comparison with these firms, twenty-nine similarly situated control firms were chosen and samples were matched by meeting the criteria above and by industry groupings. (The lists of both these experimental and control firms, with their acquisitions, are given in appendixes B and C, respectively).

The stock return data for both the excellent and control firms comes from the monthly *CRSP Files* compiled by the University of Chicago Center for Research in Security Prices, covering January 1, 1960, to December 31, 1984. The merger data have been obtained from Moody's *Industrial Manuals* covering the same time period. For merger announcements and other information, we also consulted the *Wall Street Journal Index*, 1960–1985.

## NATURE AND EXTENT OF ABNORMAL RETURNS IN THE EXCELLENT AND CONTROL FIRMS

Table 5.1 shows the monthly average abnormal returns of the total sample of twenty-nine firms for both the excellent and control groups of firms. Over the twenty-five-month observation period, the cumulative average abnormal returns (CAAR) of the excellent firms were a modest 9.04 percent, while the cumulative abnormal returns (CAAR) of the control firms for the same period were only 6.52 percent, thus indicating that the excellent firms did somewhat better than the non-excellent firms during this period. But the meager size of the gain also supports the conclusion of

**Table 5.1**
**Monthly Abnormal Returns for 29 Excellent and Control Firms**

| | Excellent Firms | | | | Control Firms | | |
|---|---|---|---|---|---|---|---|
| Month | AAR | t-statistic | CAAR | Month | AAR | t-stat. | CAAR |
| -12 | -0.0063 | -0.5943 | -0.0063 | -12 | 0.0199 | 1.3178 | 0.0199 |
| -11 | 0.0090 | 0.8491 | 0.0027 | -11 | 0.6423 | 0.6423 | 0.0296 |
| -10 | 0.0297 | 2.8019*** | 0.0324 | -10 | 0.0063 | 0.4172* | 0.0359 |
| -9 | -0.0088 | -0.8302 | 0.0236 | -9 | 0.0182 | 1.2053 | 0.0541 |
| -8 | 0.0322 | 3.0377*** | 0.0548 | -8 | 0.0214 | 1.4172* | 0.0755 |
| -7 | -0.0145 | -1.3679* | 0.0413 | -7 | 0.0074 | 0.4901 | 0.0829 |
| -6 | -0.0097 | -0.9151 | 0.0316 | -6 | -0.0108 | 0.7152 | 0.0721 |
| -5 | -0.0086 | -0.8113 | 0.0230 | -5 | 0.0181 | 1.1987 | 0.0902 |
| -4 | 0.0094 | 0.8868 | 0.0324 | -4 | 0.0183 | 1.2119 | 0.1085 |
| -3 | 0.0045 | 0.4245 | 0.0369 | -3 | 0.0053 | 0.3510 | 0.1138 |
| -2 | 0.0117 | 1.1038 | 0.0486 | -2 | -0.0361 | -2.3907** | 0.0777 |
| -1 | 0.0013 | 0.1226 | 0.0499 | -1 | 0.0009 | 0.0596 | 0.0786 |
| 0 | 0.0057 | 0.5377 | 0.0556 | 0 | -0.0140 | 0.9272 | 0.0646 |
| +1 | 0.0001 | 0.0094 | 0.0557 | +1 | -0.0016 | -0.1060 | 0.0630 |
| +2 | -0.0114 | -1.0755 | 0.0443 | +2 | 0.0086 | 0.5695 | 0.0716 |
| +3 | 0.0048 | 0.4528 | 0.0491 | +3 | -0.0293 | -1.9404** | 0.0423 |
| +4 | 0.0116 | 1.0943 | 0.0607 | +4 | 0.0182 | 1.2053 | 0.0605 |
| +5 | -0.0015 | -0.1415 | 0.0592 | +5 | 0.0308 | 2.0397** | 0.0913 |
| +6 | 0.0044 | 0.4151 | 0.0636 | +6 | -0.0177 | -1.1722 | 0.0736 |
| +7 | 0.0250 | 2.3585** | 0.0886 | +7 | -0.0001 | -0.0066 | 0.0735 |
| +8 | -0.0035 | 0.3302 | 0.0851 | +8 | 0.0114 | 0.7550 | 0.0849 |
| +9 | 0.0136 | 1.2830 | 0.0987 | +9 | 0.0049 | 0.3245 | 0.0898 |
| +10 | -0.0031 | -0.2925 | 0.0956 | +10 | -0.0181 | -1.1987 | 0.0717 |
| +11 | -0.0142 | -1.3396* | 0.0814 | +11 | -0.0109 | -0.7219 | 0.0608 |
| +12 | 0.0090 | 0.8491 | 0.0904 | +12 | 0.0044 | 0.2914 | 0.0652 |

* Significant at the 10% level.
** Significant at the 5% level.
*** Significant at the 1% level.

the majority of studies that the stockholders of the acquiring firms gain only modestly, and in most cases not at all, in the long run.

That the stock market is semi-strongly perfect—marked by insider trading and other abuses where any information regarding impending mergers and acquisitions is leaked out months before the event date—is borne out by our study. The gain in the event month for the excellent firms was slight, while for the control firms it was $-0.40$ percent for the same month. But the cumulative average abnormal returns of the excellent firms in the months prior to the event, particularly from month $-4$ through month $-2$ were 2.56 percent, while for the control firms, the cumulative gain was 4.17 percent from month $-5$ through month $-2$. After the event month, there were 5 months out of the twelve-month period when the abnormal returns were negative for the excellent firms, while for the control firms, the number of months with negative abnormal returns was 6 for the same period.

When we compute the cumulative average abnormal returns (CAAR) for selected intervals, as shown in table 5.2, we find that from month $-12$ through month $-1$, the CAAR of the control firms was higher than that of the excellent firms, as was also true from month $-12$ through month $+6$. But the cumulative gains after the eleventh month were higher for the excellent firms than for the control firms, as seen for both month $+2$

**Table 5.2**
**Cumulative Average Abnormal Returns for 29 Excellent and Control Firms over Selected Intervals**

| Excellent Firms | | | Control Firms | | |
|---|---|---|---|---|---|
| Interval | CAAR | t-statistic | Interval | CAAR | t-statistic |
| -12 through +12 | 0.0904 | 1.7057** | -12 through +12 | 0.0652 | 0.0636 |
| -12 through -1 | 0.0499 | 1.2569 | -12 through -1 | 0.0786 | 1.5029* |
| -12 through +6 | 0.0636 | 1.3766* | -12 through +6 | 0.0736 | 1.1185 |
| -6 through +6 | 0.0223 | 0.5838 | -6 through +6 | -0.0093 | 0.1864 |
| 0 through +1 | 0.0058 | 0.3867 | 0 through +1 | -0.0156 | -0.7290 |
| +2 through +12 | 0.0347 | 0.9858 | +2 through +12 | 0.0022 | 0.0439 |
| +6 through +12 | 0.0312 | 1.1143 | +6 through +12 | -0.0261 | -0.6541 |

\* Significant at 10% level.
\*\* Significant at 5% level.

through month +12, and month +6 through month +12. However, the higher returns experienced by the control firms during the months prior to the event date, as compared to the returns experienced by the excellent firms, indicate that the stockholders of the former group gained slightly more from merger information than did stockholders in the excellent firms.

## COMPARISON OF RETURNS IN LARGER VERSUS SMALLER ACQUISITIONS

In order to differentiate the impact between the larger and smaller acquisitions on the abnormal returns, we have divided our sample of twenty-nine firms into two groups—those that acquired firms with the book value of their stock prices equal to at least 50 percent of the acquiring firm's and those having book values of less than 50 percent of the acquiring firm's at the time they were acquired. Here, for the excellent firms, eleven firms qualified to be characterized as larger acquisitions, while the remaining eighteen firms fell into the second category, although the book values of these acquired firms were over 10 percent of the acquiring firms' book values, as noted earlier. As seen in table 5.3, stockholders in firms with larger acquisitions clearly did better than stockholders in firms with smaller acquisitions. Over the twenty-five-month observation period, firms that acquired relatively larger companies had the cumulative average abnormal returns (CAAR) of 13.70 percent, while the firms with relatively smaller acquisitions had the CAAR of 2.12 percent for the same period.

When we compare these results with the abnormal returns of the control firms, as shown in table 5.4, we find that the firms with smaller acquisitions did better, with the CAAR of 10.66 percent, as compared to 1.36 percent for firms with larger acquisitions in this group during the 25-month observation period. Obviously, the impact of larger size brought some economies of scale and other benefits pertaining to the size for the excellent firms, while for the control firms, these perceived benefits did not have any effect at all. On the contrary, paying better attention to the negotiation and the eventual management of smaller acquisitions reaped above-average returns for these nonexcellent firms.

When we compare the CAAR between these two groups over the selected intervals, as shown in table 5.5, we notice that during the twelve-month period prior to the event month, firms with larger acquisitions had much higher CAAR than firms with smaller acquisitions in the excellent group, while firms with smaller acquisitions had higher CAAR in the control group. The same was true for the excellent firms during month −6 through

**Table 5.3**
**Monthly Abnormal Returns from Larger and Smaller Acquisitions by the Excellent Firms**

| | Larger Acquisitions (11 Obs.) | | | | Smaller Acquisitions (18 Obs.) | | |
|---|---|---|---|---|---|---|---|
| Month | ARR | t-stat. | CAAR | Month | AAR | t-stat. | CAAR |
| -12 | -0.0293 | -2.7641*** | -0.0293 | -12 | 0.0078 | 0.7358 | 0.0078 |
| -11 | 0.0063 | 0.5943 | -0.0230 | -11 | 0.0105 | 0.9906 | 0.0183 |
| -10 | 0.0418 | 3.9434*** | 0.0188 | -10 | 0.0224 | 2.1132** | 0.0407 |
| -9 | -0.0208 | 1.9623** | -0.0020 | -9 | -0.0016 | -0.1509 | 0.0391 |
| -8 | 0.0191 | 1.8019** | 0.0171 | -8 | 0.0401 | 3.7830*** | 0.0792 |
| -7 | 0.0012 | 0.0012 | 0.0183 | -7 | -0.0241 | -2.2736 | 0.0551 |
| -6 | -0.0080 | 0.7547 | 0.0103 | -6 | -0.0107 | -0.0094 | 0.0444 |
| -5 | 0.0079 | 0.7453 | 0.0182 | -5 | -0.0186 | -1.7547** | 0.0258 |
| -4 | 0.0251 | 2.3679** | 0.0433 | -4 | -0.0002 | 0.0188 | 0.0256 |
| -3 | 0.0093 | 0.8774 | 0.0526 | -3 | 0.0016 | 0.1509 | 0.0272 |
| -2 | 0.0582 | 5.4906*** | 0.1108 | -2 | -0.0167 | -1.5754* | 0.0105 |
| -1 | 0.0048 | 0.4528 | 0.1156 | -1 | -0.0009 | -0.0849 | 0.0096 |
| 0 | -0.0177 | -1.6698* | 0.0979 | 0 | -0.0200 | -1.8868** | -0.0104 |
| +1 | -0.0066 | -0.6226 | 0.0913 | +1 | 0.0042 | 0.3962 | -0.0062 |
| +2 | -0.0428 | -4.0377*** | 0.0485 | +2 | 0.0078 | 0.7358 | 0.0016 |
| +3 | 0.0029 | 0.2736 | 0.0514 | +3 | 0.0059 | 0.5566 | 0.0075 |
| +4 | 0.0173 | 1.6321* | 0.0687 | +4 | 0.0080 | 0.7547 | 0.0155 |
| +5 | -0.0013 | -0.1226 | 0.0674 | +5 | -0.0017 | -0.1604 | 0.0138 |
| +6 | 0.0271 | 2.5566*** | 0.0945 | +6 | -0.0095 | -0.8962 | 0.0043 |
| +7 | 0.0393 | 3.7075*** | 0.1338 | +7 | 0.0163 | 1.5377* | 0.0206 |
| +8 | -0.0122 | -1.1509 | 0.1216 | +8 | 0.0018 | 0.1698 | 0.0224 |
| +9 | 0.0195 | 1.8396** | 0.1411 | +9 | 0.0099 | 0.9151 | 0.0323 |
| +10 | -0.-239 | -2.2547** | 0.1172 | +10 | 0.0095 | 0.8962 | 0.0418 |
| +11 | -0.0001 | -0.0094 | 0.1171 | +11 | -0.0229 | -2.1614** | 0.0189 |
| +12 | 0.0199 | 1.8774** | 0.1370 | +12 | 0.0023 | 0.2170 | 0.0212 |

\* Significant at the 10% level.
\*\* Significant at the 5% level.
\*\*\* Significant at the 1% level.

**Table 5.4**
**Monthly Abnormal Returns from Larger and Smaller Acquisitions by the Control Firms**

| Larger Acquisitions (13 Obs.) | | | | Smaller Acquisitions (16 Obs.) | | | |
|---|---|---|---|---|---|---|---|
| Month | ARR | t-stat. | CAAR | Month | ARR | t-stat. | CAAR |
| -12 | 0.0198 | 1.3179* | 0.0198 | -12 | 0.0200 | 1.3245* | 0.0200 |
| -11 | 0.0067 | 0.4437 | 0.0265 | -11 | 0.0121 | 0.8013 | 0.0321 |
| -10 | 0.0119 | 0.7881 | 0.0384 | -10 | 0.0017 | 0.1126 | 0.0338 |
| -9 | 0.0094 | 0.6225 | 0.0478 | -9 | 0.0253 | 1.6755* | 0.0591 |
| -8 | 0.0174 | 1.1324 | 0.0652 | -8 | 0.0246 | 1.6291* | 0.0837 |
| -7 | 0.0141 | 0.9338 | 0.0793 | -7 | 0.0019 | 0.1258 | 0.0856 |
| -6 | -0.0456 | -3.0199*** | 0.0337 | -6 | 0.0175 | 1.0870 | 0.1031 |
| -5 | 0.0156 | 1.0331 | 0.0493 | -5 | 0.0202 | 1.3377* | 0.1233 |
| -4 | 0.0020 | 0.1324 | 0.0513 | -4 | 0.0315 | 2.0861** | 0.1548 |
| -3 | 0.0027 | 0.1788 | 0.0540 | -3 | 0.0074 | 0.4901 | 0.1622 |
| -2 | -0.0228 | -1.5099* | 0.0312 | -2 | -0.0470 | -3.1126*** | 0.1152 |
| -1 | -0.0090 | -0.5960 | 0.0222 | -1 | 0.0089 | 0.5894 | 0.1241 |
| 0 | -0.0091 | -0.6026 | 0.0131 | 0 | -0.0180 | -1.1921 | 0.1061 |
| +1 | 0.0161 | 1.0662 | 0.0292 | +1 | -0.0163 | -1.0795 | 0.0893 |
| +2 | 0.0245 | 1.6225* | 0.0537 | +2 | -0.0044 | -0.2914 | 0.0854 |
| +3 | -0.0412 | -2.7285*** | 0.0125 | +3 | -0.0195 | -1.2915 | 0.0659 |
| +4 | 0.0570 | 3.7748*** | 0.0695 | +4 | -0.0133 | -0.8808 | 0.0526 |
| +5 | 0.0030 | 0.1987 | 0.0725 | +5 | 0.0534 | 3.5364*** | 0.1060 |
| +6 | -0.0214 | -1.4172* | 0.0511 | +6 | -0.0147 | -0.9735 | 0.0913 |
| +7 | -0.0235 | -1.5563* | 0.0276 | +7 | 0.0189 | 1.2517 | 0.1102 |
| +8 | -0.0052 | -0.3444 | 0.0254 | +8 | 0.0249 | 1.6490* | 0.1351 |
| +9 | 0.0066 | 0.4371 | 0.0290 | +9 | 0.0036 | 0.2384 | 0.1387 |
| +10 | -0.0382 | -2.5298*** | -0.0092 | +10 | -0.0018 | -0.1192 | 0.1369 |
| +11 | 0.0105 | 0.6954 | 0.0013 | +11 | -0.0283 | -1.8742** | 0.1086 |
| +12 | 0.0123 | 0.8146 | 0.0136 | +12 | -0.0020 | -0.1324 | 0.1066 |

* Significant at the 10% level.
** Significant at the 5% level.
*** Significant at the 1% level.

**Table 5.5**
**Cumulative Average Abnormal Returns from Larger and Smaller Acquisitions by the Excellent and Control Firms over Selected Intervals**

| Interval | Excellent Firms | | | | Control Firms | | | |
|---|---|---|---|---|---|---|---|---|
| | Larger Acquisitions | | Smaller Acquisitions | | Larger Acquisitions | | Smaller Acquisitions | |
| | CAAR | t-stat. | CAAR | t-stat. | CAAR | t-stat. | CAAR | t-stat |
| -12 through +12 | 0.1370 | 2.5849*** | 0.0212 | 0.4000 | 0.0136 | 0.1815 | 0.1066 | 1.4119* |
| -12 through -1 | 0.1156 | 3.1498*** | 0.0096 | 0.2616 | 0.0222 | 0.4264 | 0.1241 | 2.3728* |
| -12 through +6 | 0.0945 | 2.0454** | 0.0043 | 0.0931 | 0.0511 | 0.7781 | 0.0913 | 1.3875* |
| -6 through +6 | 0.0762 | 1.9948** | -0.0508 | -1.3298* | 0.0282 | -0.5184 | 0.0057 | 0.1048 |
| 0 through +1 | -0.0243 | -1.6211* | -0.0158 | -1.0533 | 0.0070 | 0.3271 | -0.0343 | -1.6028* |
| +2 through +12 | 0.0457 | 1.2983 | 0.0274 | 0.7784 | -0.0156 | -0.3114 | 0.0168 | 0.3353 |
| +6 through +12 | 0.0696 | 2.4857** | 0.0074 | 0.2643 | -0.0589 | -1.4762* | 0.0006 | 0.0150 |

\* Significant at the 10% level.
\*\* Significant at the 5% level.
\*\*\* Significant at the 1% level.

month +6, but for firms with smaller acquisitions in the control group, the CAAR was insignificant during the same period. Also, for the twelve-month period after the announcement of mergers, the CAAR was very small for both groups, although the firms with larger acquisitions in the excellent group fared a little better when compared to the firms belonging to the control group.

## COMPARISON OF RETURNS IN CONGLOMERATE VERSUS NON-CONGLOMERATE ACQUISITIONS

We also divided our complete sample of firms into two groups—those having conglomerate acquisitions and those that acquired firms characterized by horizontal and vertical integration. There is a great deal of debate in financial and merger literature regarding the effects of conglomerate mergers on the acquiring firms. The majority of these studies have argued that since conglomerate acquisitions tend to result in less combination of real activities than non-conglomerate acquisitions, the amount of real synergy associated with conglomerates is less than that associated with non-conglomerate acquisitions. We would then expect the stockholders' returns from conglomerate acquisitions to be less than those from

**Table 5.6**
**Monthly Abnormal Returns from Conglomerate and Non-Conglomerate Acquisitions by the Excellent Firms**

| Conglomerate Acquisitions (16 Obs.) | | | | Non-conglomerate Acq. (13 Obs. | | | |
|---|---|---|---|---|---|---|---|
| Month | AAR | t-stat. | CAAR | Month | AAR | t-stat. | CAAR |
| -12 | -0.0109 | -0.0109 | -0.0109 | -12 | -0.0006 | -0.0566 | -0.0006 |
| -11 | -0.0081 | -0.7641 | -0.0191 | -11 | 0.0301 | 2.8396*** | 0.0295 |
| -10 | 0.0140 | 1.3208* | -0.0050 | -10 | 0.0491 | 4.6321*** | 0.0786 |
| -9 | -0.0016 | -1.1509 | -0.0066 | -9 | -0.0177 | -1.6698* | 0.0609 |
| -8 | 0.0290 | 2.7358*** | 0.0224 | -8 | 0.0360 | 3.3962*** | 0.0969 |
| -7 | -0.0079 | -0.7453 | 0.' 45 | -7 | -0.0226 | -2.1321** | 0.0743 |
| -6 | -0.0020 | -0.1887 | 0.0125 | -6 | -0.0191 | -1.8019** | 0.0552 |
| -5 | -0.0123 | -1.1604 | 0.0002 | -5. | -0.0040 | -0.3774 | 0.0512 |
| -4 | -0.0063 | -0.5943 | -0.0061 | -4 | 0.0287 | 2.7075*** | 0.0799 |
| -3 | 0.0040 | 0.3774 | -0.0021 | -3 | 0.0052 | 0.4906 | 0.0851 |
| -2 | 0.0090 | 0.8491 | 0.0069 | -2 | 0.0150 | 1.4151* | 0.1001 |
| -1 | 0.0092 | 0.8679 | 0.0161 | -1 | -0.0085 | -0.8019 | 0.0916 |
| 0 | 0.0089 | 0.8396 | 0.0250 | 0 | 0.0018 | 0.1698 | 0.0934 |
| +1 | -0.0009 | -0.0849 | 0.0241 | +1 | 0.0004 | 0.0377 | 0.0938 |
| +2 | 0.0007 | 0.0660 | 0.0248 | +2 | -0.0262 | -2.4717*** | 0.0676 |
| +3 | 0.0027 | 0.2547 | 0.0275 | +3 | 0.0073 | 0.6887 | 0.0749 |
| +4 | 0.0016 | 0.1509 | 0.0291 | +4 | 0.0239 | 2.2547** | 0.0988 |
| +5 | 0.0145 | 1.3679* | 0.0436 | +5 | -0.0213 | -2.0094** | 0.0775 |
| +6 | 0.0121 | 1.1415 | 0.0557 | +6 | -0.0050 | -0.4717 | 0.0725 |
| +7 | 0.0080 | 0.7547 | 0.0637 | +7 | 0.0460 | 4.3396*** | 0.1185 |
| +8 | 0.0119 | 1.0283 | 0.0756 | +8 | -0.0224 | -2.1132** | 0.0961 |
| +9 | 0.0077 | 0.7264 | 0.0833 | +9 | 0.0209 | 1.9717** | 0.1170 |
| +10 | -0.0017 | -0.1604 | 0.0816 | +10 | -0.0049 | -0.4623 | 0.1121 |
| +11 | -0.0230 | -2.1698** | 0.0586 | +11 | -0.0035 | -0.3302 | 0.1086 |
| +12 | -0.0079 | -0.7453 | 0.0507 | +12 | 0.0298 | 2.8113*** | 0.1384 |

* Significant at the 10% level.
** Significant at the 5% level.
*** Significant at the 1% level.

**Table 5.7**
**Monthly Abnormal Returns from Conglomerate and Non-Conglomerate Acquisitions by the Control Firms**

| Conglomerate Acquisitions (17 Obs.) | | | | Non-Conglomerate Acquisitions (12 Obs.) | | | |
|---|---|---|---|---|---|---|---|
| Month | AAR | t-statistic | CAAR | Month | AAR | t-statistic | CAAR |
| -12 | 0.0120 | 0.7947 | 0.0120 | -12 | 0.0311 | 2.0596** | 0.0311 |
| -11 | 0.0022 | 0.1457 | 0.0142 | -11 | 0.0203 | 1.3444* | 0.0514 |
| -10 | -0.0056 | -0.3709 | 0.0086 | -10 | 0.0232 | 1.5364* | 0.0746 |
| - 9 | 0.0042 | 0.2781 | 0.0128 | - 9 | 0.0380 | 2.5166** | 0.1126 |
| - 8 | 0.0218 | 1.4437* | 0.0346 | - 8 | 0.0209 | 1.3841* | 0.1335 |
| - 7 | 0.0146 | 0.9669 | 0.0492 | - 7 | -0.0029 | -0.1921 | 0.1306 |
| - 6 | 0.0060 | 0.3973 | 0.0552 | - 6 | -0.0346 | -2.2914** | 0.0960 |
| - 5 | 0.0202 | 1.3377* | 0.0754 | - 5 | 0.0152 | 1.0066 | 0.1112 |
| - 4 | 0.0292 | 1.9338** | 0.1046 | - 4 | 0.0027 | 0.1788 | 0.1139 |
| - 3 | -0.0049 | -0.3245 | 0.0997 | - 3 | 0.0198 | 1.3113* | 0.1337 |
| - 2 | -0.0285 | -1.8874 | 0.0712 | - 2 | -0.0470 | -3.1126*** | 0.0867 |
| - 1 | 0.0010 | 0.0662 | 0.0722 | - 1 | 0.0008 | 0.0530 | 0.0875 |
| 0 | -0.0209 | -1.3841* | 0.0513 | 0 | -0.0041 | -0.2715 | 0.0834 |
| + 1 | -0.0092 | -0.6093 | 0.0421 | + 1 | 0.0042 | 0.2781 | 0.0876 |
| + 2 | 0.0200 | 1.3245* | 0.0621 | + 2 | -0.0077 | -0.5099 | 0.0799 |
| + 3 | -0.-152 | -1.0066 | 0.0469 | + 3 | -0.0491 | -3.2517*** | 0.0308 |
| + 4 | 0.0194 | 1.2848 | 0.0663 | + 4 | 0.0165 | 1.0927 | 0.0473 |
| + 5 | 0.0393 | 2.6020*** | 0.1056 | + 5 | 0.0188 | 1.2450 | 0.0661 |
| + 6 | -0.0236 | -1.5629* | 0.0820 | + 6 | -0.0094 | -0.6225 | 0.0567 |
| + 7 | -0.0126 | -0.8344 | 0.0694 | + 7 | 0.0176 | 1.1656 | 0.0743 |
| + 8 | 0.0079 | 0.5232 | 0.0773 | + 8 | 0.0163 | 1.0795 | 0.0906 |
| + 9 | -0.0200 | -1.3245* | 0.0573 | + 9 | -0.0165 | -1.0927 | 0.0741 |
| +10 | 0.0210 | 1.3907* | 0.0783 | +10 | -0.0735 | 4.8675*** | 0.0060 |
| +11 | -0.0364 | -2.4106** | 0.0419 | +11 | 0.0253 | 1.6755* | 0.0259 |
| +12 | 0.0102 | 0.6755 | 0.0521 | +12 | -0.0038 | -0.2517 | 0.0221 |

* Significant at the 10% level.
** Significant at the 5% level.
*** Significant at the 1% level.

**Table 5.8**
**Cumulative Average Abnormal Returns from Conglomerate and Non-Conglomerate Acquisitions by the Excellent and Control Firms over Selected Intervals**

| Interval | Excellent Firms | | | | Control Firms | | | |
|---|---|---|---|---|---|---|---|---|
| | Conglomerate Acquisitions | | Non-Conglom. Acquisitions | | Conglomerate Acquisitions | | Non-Conglom. Acquisitions | |
| | CAAR | t-stat. | CAAR | t-stat. | CAAR | t-stat. | CAAR | t-stat. |
| -12 through +12 | 0.0507 | 0.9566 | 0.1384 | 2.6113*** | 0.0521 | 0.6901 | 0.0221 | 0.2927 |
| -12 through -1 | 0.0161 | 0.4387 | 0.0916 | 2.4959*** | 0.0722 | 1.3805* | 0.0875 | 1.6730* |
| -12 through +6 | 0.0557 | 1.2056 | 0.0725 | 1.5693* | 0.0820 | 1.2462 | 0.0567 | 0.8617 |
| -6 through +6 | 0.0412 | 1.0785 | -0.0018 | -0.0471 | 0.0328 | 0.6029 | -0.0739 | -1.3103* |
| 0 through +1 | 0.0080 | 0.5333 | 0.0022 | 0.1467 | -0.0301 | 1.4065* | 0.0001 | 0.0047 |
| +2 through +12 | 0.0266 | 0.7557 | 0.0446 | 1.2670 | 0.0100 | 0.1996 | -0.0655 | -1.3074* |
| +6 through +12 | 0.0071 | 0.2536 | 0.0609 | 2.1750** | -0.0535 | -1.3408 | -0.0440 | -1.1028 |

```
   *   Significant at the 10% level.
  **   Significant at the  5% level.
 ***   Significant at the  1% level.
```

non-conglomerate acquisitions, if there are no pure financial effects associated with the acquisitions. The important studies done by Mandelker, Langetieg, Dodd, and Asquith and Kim have found little evidence of greater synergy from conglomerate acquisitions.[14]

In tables 5.6 and 5.7, we have shown the average abnormal returns and the cumulative average abnormal returns of firms with conglomerate acquisitions, as compared to firms with non-conglomerate acquisitions, for both the excellent and the control groups. Here, also, the results are mixed. For the excellent firms, the CAAR of sixteen firms with conglomerate acquisitions was 5.07 percent during the observation period, while thirteen firms with non-conglomerate acquisitions had a CAAR of 13.84 percent, almost two and a half times higher than the former group. But for the control firms, those seventeen firms with the conglomerate acquisitions had a CAAR of 5.21 percent, while the remaining twelve firms with non-conglomerate acquisitions had a CAAR of a meager 2.21 percent for the same period. Obviously, no real synergies were realized by the firms with conglomerate acquisitions as compared to non-conglomerate acquisitions among the excellent firms, while for the firms with conglomerate acquisitions in the control group there was only a very modest gain during the entire observation period.

As for the CAAR over selected intervals, as shown in table 5.8, we find that for the twelve-month period prior to the event month, firms with conglomerate acquisitions in the excellent group gained an insignificant 1.61 percent, while the firms with conglomerate acquisitions in the control group gained a modest 7.22 percent. The gains for firms with non-conglomerate acquisitions were virtually the same for both groups. But from month −6 through month +6, firms in the excellent group with conglomerate acquisitions did slightly better than their counterparts, while the CAAR of the control firms with non-conglomerate acquisitions, for the same period, was negative. The same was true for the period from month +2 through month +12, whereas for the period from month +6 through +12 the CAAR in the control group was negative for both types of acquisitions. Thus the excellent firms did somewhat better as compared to the control firms, but mainly by non-conglomerate acquisitions, and not by acquisitions of the conglomerate variety.[15]

## NOTES

1. G. Mandelker, "Risk and Return: The Case of Merging Firms," *Journal of Financial Economics,* Vol. 1 (Dec. 1974): 303–35.

2. J. R. Franks, J. E. Broyles, and M. J. Hecht, "An Industry Study of the Profitability of Mergers in the United Kingdom," *Journal of Finance,* Vol. 32 (Dec. 1977): 1513–25.

3. J. C. Ellert, "Mergers, Antitrust Law Enforcement, and Stochastic Returns," *Journal of Finance,* Vol. 31 (May 1976): 715–32.

4. P. R. Dodd and R. Ruback, "Tender Offers and Stockholders' Returns: An Empirical Analysis," *Journal of Financial Economics,* Vol. 5 (December 1977), no. 3: 351–74; see also P. R. Dodd, "Merger Proposals, Management Discretion and Stockholder Wealth," *Journal of Financial Economics,* Vol. 8 (June 1980): 105–37.

5. P. Halpern, "Empirical Estimates of the Amount and Distribution of Gains to Companies in Mergers," *Journal of Business,* Vol. 46 (Oct. 1973): 554–73.

6. S. R. Reid, *Mergers, Managers and the Economy* (New York: McGraw-Hill, 1968), pp. 153–69.

7. T. F. Hogarty, "The Profitability of Corporate Mergers," *Journal of Business,* Vol. 43 (July 1970): 317–27.

8. R. A. Shick and F. C. Jen, "Merger Benefits to Shareholders of Acquiring Firms," *Financial Management,* Vol. 3 (Winter 1974): 45–53.

9. T. Langetieg, "An Application of a Three-Factor Performance Index to Measure Stockholder Gains from Merger," *Journal of Financial Economics,* Vol. 6 (Dec. 1978): 365–83.

10. P. Asquith, "Merger Bids, Market Uncertainty, and Stockholder Returns," *Journal of Financial Economics,* Vol. 11 (April 1983): 51–83; see also P. Asquith and E. H. Kim, "The Impact of Merger Bids on the Participating Firms' Security Holders," *Journal of Finance,* Vol. 37 (Dec. 1982): 1209–28.

11. E. Fama et al.; "The Adjustment of Stock Prices for New Information," *International Economic Review,* Vol. 1 (Feb. 1969): 1–21.

12. S. Brown and J. Warner, "Measuring Security Price Performance," *Journal of Financial Economics,* Vol. 8 (September 1980): 205–58.

13. P. C. Jain, "The Effect of Voluntary Sell-off Announcements on Shareholders' Wealth," *Journal of Finance,* Vol. 40 (March 1985): 209–24.

14. G. Mandelker, "Risk and Return: The Case of Merging Firm," pp. 316–24; T. C. Langetieg, "An Application of a Three-factor Performance Index to Measure Stockholder Gains from Merger," pp. 371–81; P. Dodd, "Merger Proposals, Management Discretion and Stockholder Wealth," pp. 105–37; Paul Asquith and E. Han Kim, "The Impact of Merger Bids on the Participating Firms' Security Holders," pp. 1222–27.

15. Arabinda Ghosh, "Corporate Acquisitions and Stockholders' Returns in the United States Excellent Firms," *North American Review of Economics and Finance,* Vol. 1 (December 1988): 101–29. This chapter originally appeared in this journal; permission to publish here is gratefully acknowledged.

# 6

# Divestitures and Stockholders' Wealth in the United States' Excellent Firms

In this chapter, we want to examine whether shareholders of the excellent firms earned higher positive abnormal returns than those investing in the non-excellent firms when these firms went into voluntary sell-offs during 1960–1984. The finance literature is generally unanimous in the conclusion that the shareholders of the divesting firm earn positive abnormal returns. Boudreaux found a positive stock price effect for spin-offs and sell-offs together for the divesting firms up to three months around the event date.[1] Alexander et al. examined a sample of fifty-three firms and found positive but small abnormal returns to the stockholders of the selling firms.[2] Jain found that both the sellers and buyers earned significant positive abnormal returns around the time of sell-off announcements.[3] Klein also found that on average, an initial sell-off announcement results in a significant but small positive average abnormal return for the selling firm.[4] It would therefore be worthwhile to ask if the stockholders of the United States' excellent firms attained any above-average returns from the sell-offs during 1960–1984.

The research methodology we follow here is again that of the event studies as developed in finance. There are generally two ways of calculating the average abnormal returns (AAR): the mean-adjusted return approach and the market-adjusted return approach. In chapter 5, we used the market-adjusted return approach. In order to compare the results pursuing different methodology, we will follow here the mean-adjusted return approach.

The mean-adjusted return approach was used very successfully by Brown and Warner to compute the average abnormal returns.[5] This study shows that the mean-adjusted model performs as well as the more sophisticated market model in detecting abnormal returns when they are present. To determine the monthly abnormal returns of a security, we first calculate the average monthly return over a specified interval—the comparison period. This comparison period return (CPR) is taken as an estimate of the expected monthly return for the period under study—the observation period. The CPR for our comparison period calculation was based on the average monthly returns from $-48$ month through $-13$ month, totaling 36 months. The observation period extends for $-12$ month through $+12$ month. The average abnormal return (AAR) is obtained for each month over the twenty-five-month observation period by using the formula:

$$AAR_n = \frac{\sum_{j=1}^{n} a_{jm}}{n} \tag{1}$$

where:

$$n = \text{number of sample securities,}$$
$$a_{jm} = \text{abnormal return for security } j \text{ on month } m,$$
$$AAR_m = \text{average abnormal return for month } m.$$

The cumulative average abnormal return (CAAR) for month $m$ is defined by:

$$CAAR_m = \sum_{k=-12}^{m} AAR_k \tag{2}$$

A $t$-statistic that tests whether the average abnormal return for month $m$ is significantly different than zero is calculated, following Jain, by:

$$t_m = AAR_m/s \tag{3}$$

where $s$ is the estimated standard deviation of the $AAR_s$ calculated from the comparison period (month $-48$ to month $-13$) relative to the event month for each firm. Similarly, the $t$-statistic of CAAR for a period of $N$ months from month $a$ to month $b$ is calculated by:

$$t_{ab} = CAAR_{ab}/s\sqrt{n} \tag{4}$$

## HYPOTHESIS TESTING OF SELL-OFFS BY
## THE EXCELLENT AND CONTROL FIRMS

There are many reasons why a firm engages in a voluntary sell-off and why the shareholders of the selling firm may expect to gain from it. First, a divestiture may eliminate negative synergies, and a sell-off, by rectifying the misallocation of resources and thereby increasing future cash-flows, may increase the value of the firm. Second, a sell-off can be viewed as a partial merger, as Jain has pointed out. If certain parts of the firm are more valuable to the outsiders than to the present owners, it is in the shareholders' interest to divest themselves of these assets, in which case the market should react favorably to the sellers' stock price around the announcement dates. Third, like spin-off, a sell-off may result in the desire of the selling firm to specialize in a limited number of business activities, resulting in a positive stock price reaction. Finally, following the agency theory in finance, a sell-off may be undertaken in order to transfer wealth where shareholders are paid dividends from the proceeds of the sale of assets, thus reducing the probable payments to the bondholders and in turn, increasing the common stock values of the selling firm.[6]

We have taken the divestiture activites of those firms that were listed as excellent in Peters and Waterman's book *In Search of Excellence* (see table 1.1). Out of the 62 U.S. firms, 56 were public companies and 53 belonged to the New York Stock Exchange. We have taken the NYSE firms that met the following two criteria:

1. The selling firms were engaged in a major divestiture between January 1, 1960, and December 31, 1984; and

2. The selling firm had no other merger or divestiture for one year preceding and one year after the announcement of the divestiture, so that the full impact of the divestiture on stock returns might be investigated.

Only twenty-two excellent firms met these requirements. For our comparison with these excellent firms, nineteen similarly situated control firms (which were matched with the former group in their respective industries, and met the above criteria) were chosen.

The stock return data for both the excellent and control firms come from the monthly *CRSP Files* compiled by the University of Chicago Center for Research in Security Prices, covering January 1, 1957, to December 31, 1984. The sell-off data were obtained from Moody's *Industrial Manuals* covering 1960–1984. For the initial public announcements of the divestitures we also consulted the *Wall Street Journal Index,* 1960–1985.

**Table 6.1**
**Monthly Average Abnormal Returns for 22 Excellent Firms**

| Month | AAR | t-statistic | CAAR |
|-------|-----|-------------|------|
| -12 | 0.0321 | 2.5887** | 0.0321 |
| -11 | 0.0236 | 1.9032** | 0.0557 |
| -10 | 0.0169 | 1.3629 | 0.0726 |
| -9 | 0.0032 | 0.2581 | 0.0758 |
| -8 | -0.0150 | -1.2097 | 0.0608 |
| -7 | -0.0416 | -3.3548** | 0.0192 |
| -6 | -0.0291 | -2.3468* | -0.0099 |
| -5 | -0.0068 | -0.5484 | -0.0167 |
| -4 | -0.0326 | -2.6290 | -0.0493 |
| -3 | -0.0453 | -3.6532** | -0.0946 |
| -2 | -0.-235 | -1.8952* | -0.1181 |
| -1 | 0.0318 | 2.5645** | -0.0863 |
| 0 | 0.0211 | 1.7016 | -0.0652 |
| +1 | -0.0102 | -0.8226 | -0.0754 |
| +2 | 0.0078 | 0.6290 | -0.0676 |
| +3 | 0.0423 | 3.4113** | -0.0253 |
| +4 | -0.0177 | -1.4274 | -0.0430 |
| +5 | -0.0198 | -1.5968 | -0.0628 |
| +6 | -0.0396 | -3.1935** | -0.1024 |
| +7 | -0.0258 | -2.0806* | -0.1282 |
| +8 | -0.0059 | -0.4758 | -0.1341 |
| +9 | -0.0194 | -1.5645 | -0.1535 |
| +10 | -0.0136 | -1.0968 | -0.1671 |
| +11 | -0.0105 | -0.8468 | -0.1776 |
| +12 | 0.0051 | 0.4113 | -0.1725 |

* Significant at the 5% level.
** Significant at the 1% level.

**Table 6.2**
**Monthly Average Abnormal Returns for 19 Control Firms**

| Month | AAR | t-statistic | CAAR |
|---|---|---|---|
| -12 | -0.0090 | -0.6294 | -0.0090 |
| -11 | -0.0097 | -0.6783 | -0.0187 |
| -10 | -0.0025 | -0.1748 | -0.0212 |
| -9 | 0.0146 | 1.0210 | -0.0061 |
| -8 | 0.0005 | 0.0350 | -0.0174 |
| -7 | -0.0113 | -0.7902 | -0.0174 |
| -6 | 0.0335 | 2.3427* | 0.0161 |
| -5 | -0.0082 | -0.5734 | 0.0079 |
| -4 | 0.0018 | 0.1259 | 0.0097 |
| -3 | -0.0132 | -0.9231 | -0.0035 |
| -2 | -0.0188 | -1.3147 | -0.0223 |
| -1 | 0.0115 | 0.8042 | -0.0108 |
| 0 | 0.0098 | 0.6853 | -0.0010 |
| +1 | 0.0151 | 1.0559 | 0.0141 |
| +2 | -0.0071 | -0.4965 | 0.0070 |
| +3 | -0.0440 | -3.0769** | -0.0370 |
| +4 | 0.0101 | 0.7133 | -0.0268 |
| +5 | -0.0133 | -0.9301 | -0.0401 |
| +6 | -0.0353 | -2.4686* | -0.0754 |
| +7 | -0.0229 | -1.6014 | 0.0983 |
| +8 | 0.0279 | 1.9510 | -0.0704 |
| +9 | 0.0035 | 0.2448 | -0.0669 |
| +10 | -0.0198 | -1.3846 | -0.0867 |
| +11 | -0.0341 | -2.3846* | -0.1208 |
| +12 | 0.0126 | 0.8811 | -0.1082 |

* Significant at the 5% level.
** Significant at the 1% level.

## DIVESTITURES AND STOCKHOLDERS' RETURNS IN
## THE EXCELLENT AND CONTROL FIRMS

In table 6.1 we have shown the monthly average abnormal returns of the total sample of twenty-two excellent firms. Over the twenty-five-month observation period, the cumulative average abnormal return (CAAR) was −17.25 percent, indicating the general bear market of the 1970s. But the important fact is that the average abnormal returns (AAR) surrounding the event month were positive, as the theory would predict, and the *t*-value for 0 month and −1 month were significant at 10 percent and 5 percent levels, respectively. Table 6.1 also confirms the finding of Alexander et al. that the average abnormal returns are mostly negative in the months preceding and succeeding the event date.

When we compare these results with the results obtained for the nineteen control firms, as shown in table 6.2, we find that the cumulative average abnormal returns (CAAR) for the latter group, although negative, were of lower value than those of the excellent firms, thus indicating that the control firms performed relatively better than the excellent firms in this respect. Here, also, the average abnormal returns for 0 month and −1 month were positive, although they were not significant statistically. Thus, in spite of the overall negative returns for the entire twenty-five-month period, both the excellent and the control firms had positive abnormal returns around the time of the sell-off announcements.

In table 6.3, we have computed the cumulative average abnormal returns (CAAR) for selected intervals. Here we find that for both the periods covering

**Table 6.3**
**Cumulative Average Abnormal Returns for the Excellent and Control Firms over Selected Intervals**

| Excellent Firms | | | Control Firms | | |
|---|---|---|---|---|---|
| Interval | CAAR | t-stat. | Interval | CAAR | t-stat. |
| -12 through +12 | -0.1725 | -2.7823** | -12 through +12 | -0.1082 | -1.5133 |
| -12 through -1 | -0.0863 | -2.0117* | -12 through -1 | -0.0108 | -0.2182 |
| -12 through +6 | -0.1024 | -1.8928* | -12 through +6 | -0.0754 | -1.2103 |
| -6 through +6 | -0.1216 | -2.7204** | -6 through +6 | -0.0580 | -1.1240 |
| -1 through 0 | 0.0529 | 3.0229* | -1 through 0 | 0.0213 | 1.0545 |
| +2 through +12 | -0.0971 | -2.3650* | +2 through +12 | -0.1223 | -2.5802* |
| +6 through +12 | -0.1097 | -3.3445** | +6 through +12 | -0.0681 | -1.8016 |

* Significant at the 5% level.

** Significant at the 1% level.

**Table 6.4**
**Monthly Average Abnormal Returns from Larger and Smaller Divestitures by the Excellent Firms**

| | Larger Divestitures (7 Obs.) | | | | Smaller Divestitures (15 Obs.) | | |
|--------|---------|-----------|---------|--------|---------|-----------|---------|
| Month | ARR | t-stat. | CAAR | Month | AAR | t-stat. | CAAR |
| -12 | -0.0173 | -1.3952 | -0.0173 | -12 | 0.0551 | 4.4435** | 0.0551 |
| -11 | 0.0642 | 5.1774** | 0.0469 | -11 | 0.0046 | 0.3710 | 0.0597 |
| -10 | 0.0510 | 4.1129** | 0.0979 | -10 | 0.0010 | 0.0806 | 0.0607 |
| -9 | 0.0492 | 3.9677** | 0.1471 | -9 | -0.0183 | -1.4758 | 0.0424 |
| -8 | -0.0469 | -3.7823** | 0.1002 | -8 | -0.0001 | -0.0081 | 0.0423 |
| -7 | -0.0420 | -3.3871** | 0.0582 | -7 | -0.0416 | -3.3548** | 0.0007 |
| -6 | -0.0062 | -0.5000 | 0.0520 | -6 | -0.0398 | -3.2097** | -0.0391 |
| -5 | -0.0033 | -0.2261 | 0.0487 | -5 | -0.0012 | -0.0968 | -0.0403 |
| -4 | -0.0802 | -6.4677** | -0.0315 | -4 | -0.0104 | -0.8387 | -0.0507 |
| -3 | -0.0388 | -3.1290** | -0.0703 | -3 | -0.0484 | -3.9032** | -0.0991 |
| -2 | -0.0340 | -2.7417 | -0.1043 | -2 | -0.0186 | -1.5000 | -0.1177 |
| -1 | 0.0575 | 4.6371** | -0.0468 | -1 | 0.0198 | 1.5968 | -0.0979 |
| 0 | 0.0211 | 1.7016 | -0.0257 | 0 | 0.0212 | 1.7097 | -0.0767 |
| +1 | -0.0359 | -2.8952* | -0.0616 | +1 | 0.0018 | 0.1452 | -0.0749 |
| +2 | 0.0288 | 2.3226* | -0.0328 | +2 | -0.0020 | -0.1613 | -0.0358 |
| +3 | 0.0450 | 3.6290** | 0.0122 | +3 | 0.0411 | 3.3145** | -0.0358 |
| +4 | -0.0121 | -0.9758 | 0.0001 | +4 | -0.0203 | -0.6371 | -0.0561 |
| +5 | -0.-596 | -4.8064** | -0.0595 | +5 | -0.0012 | 0.0968 | -0.0573 |
| +6 | -0.0766 | -6.1774** | -0.1361 | +6 | -0.0223 | -1.7984* | -0.0796 |
| +7 | -0.0329 | -2.6532* | -0.1690 | +7 | -0.0225 | -1.8145* | -0.1021 |
| +8 | 0.0548 | 4.4194** | -0.1142 | +8 | -0.0339 | -2.7339** | -0.1360 |
| +9 | 0.0183 | 1.4758 | -0.0959 | +9 | -0.0199 | -1.6048 | -0.1559 |
| +10 | -0.0064 | -0.5161 | -0.1023 | +10 | -0.0169 | -1.3629 | -0.1728 |
| +11 | -0.0219 | -1.7661 | -0.1242 | +11 | -0.--53 | -0.4274 | -0.1781 |
| +12 | -0.0053 | -0.4274 | -0.1295 | +12 | 0.0053 | 0.4274 | -0.1728 |

* Significant at the 5% level.
** Significant at the 1% level.

$-12$ month through $-1$ month, and $-12$ month through $+6$ month, the control firms performed relatively better than the excellent firms, as they had lower negative returns than the latter group. The same was true for $+2$ month through $+12$ month, as well as $+6$ month through $+12$ month.

But for the event months (months $-1$ through 0), the excellent firms had higher positive abnormal returns than the control firms.

## STOCKHOLDERS' RETURNS IN LARGER VERSUS SMALLER DIVESTITURES

Miles and Rosenfeld, and others, have found in their studies that the relative size of divestiture is important in its effect on the abnormal returns of the firms.[7] In order to differentiate the impact between the larger and smaller divestitures on the abnormal returns, we have divided our total sample of both the excellent and control firms into two subsamples—those that divested over $50 million of the book value of assests, and those that divested $50 million or less of the book value of assests at the time of their divestitures. In our subsample for the excellent firms, there were 7 firms that undertook such large divestitures, while 15 firms undertook relatively smaller divestitures of assets. For the control group, we chose 7 firms that made divestitures in the magnitude of over $50 million of their assets, and 12 firms that made relatively smaller divestitures during the same period.

Table 6.4 shows the same pattern we have witnessed in tables 6.1 and 6.2, that the cumulative average abnormal returns (CAAR) were negative for the entire twenty-five-month period for both groups. But here firms with larger divestitures performed relatively better, as their losses were less than those of firms with smaller divestitures. Also, the average abnormal returns (AAR) surrounding the event dates were positive for both groups, although they were statistically significant only for firms with larger divestitures. The result was opposite for the control firms, as seen in table 6.5, where firms with smaller divestitures performed relatively better, and where the cumulative losses were much lower than those of firms with larger divestitures. Here, also, the average abnormal return preceding the event month was posititive for firms with larger divestitures, while it was positive for the event month itself for firms with smaller divestitures.

When we compare the cumulative average abnormal returns (CAAR) for larger and smaller divestitures by both the excellent and control firms over the selected intervals, as shown in table 6.6, we find that for the period $-12$ month through $-1$ month, firms with larger divestitures performed better for both the excellent and control firms, and the latter group had a slightly positive CAAR. This was also true for the months surrounding the event date, when for the excellent firms with larger divestitures the gain was 7.86 percent, as compared to a 4.10 percent gain for the excellent firms with

**Table 6.5**
**Monthly Average Abnormal Returns from Larger and Smaller Divestitures by the Control Firms**

| Larger Divestitures (7 Obs.) | | | | Smaller Divestitures (12 Obs.) | | | |
|---|---|---|---|---|---|---|---|
| Month | AAR | t-stat. | CAAR | Month | AAR | t-stat. | CAAR |
| -12 | 0.0197 | 1.3776 | 0.0197 | -12 | -0.0257 | -1.7972* | -0.0257 |
| -11 | 0.0151 | 1.0559 | 0.0348 | -11 | -0.0241 | -1.6853 | -0.0498 |
| -10 | 0.0030 | 0.2098 | 0.0378 | -10 | -0.0057 | -0.3986 | -0.0555 |
| - 9 | -0.0148 | -1.1935 | 0.0230 | - 9 | 0.0317 | 2.2168* | -0.0238 |
| - 8 | -0.0266 | -2.1451* | -0.0036 | - 8 | 0.0164 | 1.1469 | -0.0074 |
| - 7 | 0.0120 | 0.8392 | 0.0084 | - 7 | -0.0249 | -1.7413 | -0.0323 |
| - 6 | 0.0267 | 1.8671 | 0.0351 | - 6 | 0.0375 | 2.6224* | -0.0052 |
| - 5 | 0.0043 | 0.3007 | 0.0394 | - 5 | -0.0155 | -1.0839 | -0.0103 |
| - 4 | -0.0090 | -0.6294 | 0.0304 | - 4 | 0.0082 | 0.5734 | -0.0021 |
| - 3 | -0.0192 | -1.3427 | 0.0112 | - 3 | -0.0097 | -0.6783 | -0.0118 |
| - 2 | -0.0204 | -1.4266 | -0.0092 | - 2 | -0.0179 | -1.2517 | -0.0297 |
| - 1 | 0.0475 | 3.3217** | 0.0383 | - 1 | -0.0095 | -0.6643 | -0.0392 |
| 0 | -0.0209 | -1.4615 | 0.0174 | 0 | 0.0277 | 1.9371* | -0.0115 |
| + 1 | 0.0181 | 1.2657 | 0.0355 | + 1 | 0.0134 | 0.9371 | 0.0019 |
| + 2 | 0.0016 | 0.1119 | 0.0371 | + 2 | -0.0121 | -0.8462 | -0.0102 |
| + 3 | -0.0856 | -5.9860** | -0.0485 | + 3 | -0.0198 | -1.3846 | -0.0300 |
| + 4 | -0.0373 | -2.6084* | -0.0858 | + 4 | 0.0379 | 2.6503 | 0.0079 |
| + 5 | -0.0247 | -1.7273 | -0.1105 | + 5 | -0.0066 | -0.4615 | 0.0013 |
| + 6 | 0.0040 | 0.2797 | -0.1065 | + 6 | -0.0583 | -4.0769** | -0.0570 |
| + 7 | -0.-492 | -3.4406** | -0.1557 | + 7 | -0.0076 | -0.5315 | -0.0646 |
| + 8 | -0.0254 | -1.7762 | -0.1811 | + 8 | 0.0590 | 4.1259** | -0.0056 |
| + 9 | 0.0199 | 1.3916 | -0.1612 | + 9 | -0.0060 | -0.4196 | -0.0116 |
| +10 | -0.-368 | -2.5734* | -0.1980 | +10 | -0.0099 | -0.6923 | -0.0215 |
| +11 | -0.0088 | -0.6154 | -0.2068 | +11 | -0.0490 | -3.4266** | -0.0705 |
| +12 | 0.0012 | 0.0839 | -0.2056 | +12 | 0.0192 | 1.3427 | -0.0513 |

\* Significant at the 5% level.
\*\* Significant at the 1% level.

**Table 6.6**

**Cumulative Average Abnormal Returns from Larger and Smaller Divestitures by the Excellent and Control Firms over Selected Intervals**

| | Excellent Firms | | | | Control Firms | | | |
|---|---|---|---|---|---|---|---|---|
| | Larger Divestiture | | Smaller Divestiture | | Larger Divestiture | | Smaller Divestiture | |
| Interval | CAAR | t-stat. | CAAR | t-stat. | CAAR | t-stat | CAAR | t-stat. |
| -12 through -12 | -0.1295 | -0.0887* | -0.1728 | -2.7871** | -0.2056 | -2.8755** | -0.0513 | -0.7175 |
| -12 through -1 | -0.0468 | -1.0909 | -0.0979 | -2.2821* | 0.0383 | 0.7737 | -0.0392 | -0.7919 |
| -12 through -6 | -0.1361 | -1.8928 | -0.0796 | -1.4713 | -0.1065 | -1.7095 | -0.0570 | -0.9149 |
| -6 through -6 | -0.1943 | -4.3468** | -0.1082 | -2.2998* | -0.1149 | -2.2267* | 0.0247 | 0.4787 |
| -1 through 0 | 0.0786 | 4.4914* | 0.0410 | 2.4329 | 0.0266 | 1.3168 | 0.0182 | 0.9010 |
| +2 through +12 | -0.0679 | -1.6520 | -0.0979 | -2.3820* | -0.2411 | -5.0865** | -0.0532 | -1.1224 |
| -6 through +12 | -0.0700 | -2.1341* | -0.1155 | -3.5213 | -0.0951 | -2.5159** | -0.0526 | -1.3915 |

\* Significant at the 5% level.
\*\* Significant at the 1% level.

smaller divestitures for the two-month period. The returns were also positive for this period for the control firms with both larger and smaller divestitures, although they were not statistically significant. But for +2 month through +12 month, the cumulative average abnormal returns were highly negative for the control firms with larger divestitures, although for the excellent firms for the same period they were less negative, even when compared to the firms with smaller divestitures belonging to the same group.

## STOCKHOLDERS' RETURNS IN PRICE DISCLOSURES VERSUS NON-PRICE DISCLOSURES

Klein has pointed out the differential impact of the public announcement of transaction prices in divestitures on shareholder wealth.[8] She found the announcement day effect to be significantly positive for the price group, but not statistically different than zero for the no-price group. We find evidence to the contrary. As shown in table 6.7, the negative value of the CAAR for the excellent firms with unannounced transaction prices was lower than that for the announced price group. Not only that, but the

**Table 6.7**
**Monthly Average Abnormal Returns from Announced and Unannounced Transaction Prices by the Excellent Firms**

| Unannounced Price Group (11 Obs.) | | | | Announced Price Group (11 Obs.) | | | |
|---|---|---|---|---|---|---|---|
| Month | AAR | t-stat. | CAAR | Month | AAR | t-stat. | CAAR |
| -12 | 0.0267 | 2.1532* | 0.0267 | -12 | 0.0375 | 3.0242** | 0.0375 |
| -11 | 0.0027 | 0.2177 | 0.0294 | -11 | 0.0445 | 3.5887** | 0.0820 |
| -10 | 0.0215 | 1.7339 | 0.0509 | -10 | 0.0123 | 0.9919 | 0.0943 |
| -9 | -0.0209 | -1.6855 | 0.0300 | -9 | 0.0273 | 2.2016* | 0.1216 |
| -8 | 0.0167 | 1.3468 | 0.0467 | -8 | -0.0466 | -3.7581** | 0.0750 |
| -7 | -0.0561 | -4.5242** | -0.0094 | -7 | -0.0274 | -2.2097* | 0.0476 |
| -6 | -0.0468 | -3.7742** | -0.0562 | -6 | -0.0114 | -0.9194 | 0.0362 |
| -5 | 0.0055 | 0.4435 | -0.0507 | -5 | -0.0192 | -1.5484 | 0.0170 |
| -4 | -0.0031 | -0.2500 | -0.0538 | -4 | -0.0620 | -5.0000** | -0.0450 |
| -3 | -0.0441 | -3.5565** | -0.0979 | -3 | -0.0466 | 3.7581** | -0.0916 |
| -2 | -0.0251 | -2.0242* | -0.1230 | -2 | -0.0218 | -1.7581 | -0.1134 |
| -1 | -0.0011 | -0.0887 | -0.1241 | -1 | 0.0647 | 5.2177** | -0.0487 |
| 0 | 0.0558 | 4.5000** | -0.0683 | 0 | -0.0135 | -1.0887 | -0.0622 |
| +1 | 0.0209 | 1.6855 | -0.0474 | +1 | -0.0413 | -3.3301** | -0.1035 |
| +2 | 0.0019 | 0.1532 | -0.0455 | +2 | 0.0138 | 1.1129 | -0.0897 |
| +3 | 0.0112 | 0.9032 | -0.0343 | +3 | 0.0734 | 5.9193** | -0.0163 |
| +4 | -0.0156 | -1.2581 | -0.0499 | +4 | -0.0199 | -1.6048 | -0.0362 |
| +5 | 0.0101 | 0.8145 | -0.0398 | +5 | -0.0587 | -4.7339** | -0.0949 |
| +6 | -0.0030 | -0.2419 | -0.0428 | +6 | -0.0762 | -6.1452** | -0.1711 |
| +7 | -0.0084 | -0.6774 | -0.0512 | +7 | -0.0432 | -3.4839** | -0.2143 |
| +8 | -0.0467 | -3.7661** | -0.0979 | +8 | 0.0349 | 2.8145** | -0.1794 |
| +9 | -0.0452 | -3.6452** | -0.1431 | +9 | 0.0064 | 0.5161 | -0.1730 |
| +10 | -0.0196 | -1.5806 | -0.1627 | +10 | -0.0075 | -0.6048 | -0.1805 |
| +11 | -0.0001 | -0.0081 | -0.1628 | +11 | -0.0209 | -1.6855 | -0.2014 |
| +12 | 0.0343 | 2.7661** | -0.1285 | +12 | -0.0241 | -1.9435* | -0.2255 |

* Significant at the 5% level.
** Significant at the 1% level.

**Table 6.8**
**Monthly Average Abnormal Returns from Announced and Unannounced**
**Transaction Prices by the Control Firms**

| Unannounced Price Group (9 Obs.) | | | | Announced Price Group (10 Obs.) | | | |
|---|---|---|---|---|---|---|---|
| Month | AAR | t-stat. | CAAR | Month | AAR | t-stat. | CAAR |
| -12 | -0.0202 | -1.4126 | -0.0202 | -12 | 0.0011 | 0.0769 | 0.0011 |
| -11 | -0.0088 | 0.6154 | -0.0290 | -11 | -0.0104 | -0.7273 | -0.0093 |
| -10 | -0.0022 | -0.1538 | -0.0312 | -10 | -0.0027 | -0.1888 | -0.0120 |
| -9 | 0.0545 | 3.8112** | 0.0233 | -9 | -0.0213 | -1.4895 | -0.0333 |
| -8 | 0.0372 | 2.6014* | 0.0605 | -8 | -0.0325 | -2.2727* | -0.0658 |
| -7 | -0.0275 | -1.9231* | 0.0330 | -7 | 0.0032 | 0.2238 | -0.0626 |
| -6 | 0.0468 | 3.2727** | 0.0798 | -6 | 0.0216 | 1.5105 | -0.0410 |
| -5 | -0. 0030 | -0.2308 | 0.0768 | -5 | 0.0129 | 0.9021 | -0.0281 |
| -4 | -0.0098 | -0.6853 | 0.0670 | -4 | 0.0123 | 0.8601 | -0.0158 |
| -3 | -0.0130 | -0.9091 | 0.0540 | -3 | -0.0133 | -0.9301 | -0.0291 |
| -2 | -0.0067 | -0.4685 | 0.0473 | -2 | -0.0297 | -2.0769* | -0.0588 |
| -1 | 0.0128 | 0.8951 | 0.0601 | -1 | 0.0103 | 0.7203 | -0.0485 |
| 0 | 0.0351 | 2.4545* | 0.0952 | 0 | -0.0130 | -0.9091 | -0.0615 |
| +1 | 0.0095 | 0.6643 | 0.1047 | +1 | 0.0201 | 1.4056 | -0.0414 |
| +2 | -0.0181 | -1.2657 | 0.0866 | +2 | 0.0028 | 0.1958 | -0.0386 |
| +3 | -0.0135 | -0.9441 | 0.0731 | +3 | -0.0715 | -5.0000** | -0.1101 |
| +4 | 0.0446 | 3.1189** | 0.1177 | +4 | -0.0208 | -1.4545 | -0.1309 |
| +5 | -0.0201 | -1.4056 | 0.0976 | +5 | -0.0071 | -0.4965 | -0.1380 |
| +6 | -0.0578 | -4.0419** | 0.0398 | +6 | -0.0151 | -1.0559 | -0.1531 |
| +7 | 0.0199 | 1.3916 | 0.0597 | +7 | -0.0615 | -4.3007** | -0.2146 |
| +8 | 0.0464 | 3.2448** | 0.1061 | +8 | 0.0113 | 0.7902 | -0.2033 |
| +9 | 0.0037 | 0.2587 | 0.1098 | +9 | 0.0033 | 0.2308 | -0.2000 |
| +10 | 0.0005 | 0.0350 | 0.1103 | +10 | -0.0381 | -2.6643* | -0.2381 |
| +11 | -0.0345 | -2.4126* | 0.0758 | +11 | -0.0339 | -2.3706* | -0.2720 |
| +12 | 0.0025 | 0.1748 | 0.0783 | +12 | 0.0217 | 1.5175 | -0.2503 |

*Significant at the 5% level.
**Significant at the 1% level.

**Table 6.9**
**Cumulative Average Abnormal Returns for Unannounced and Announced Divestitures
by the Excellent and Control Firms over Selected Intervals**

| | Excellent Firms | | | | Control Firms | | | |
|---|---|---|---|---|---|---|---|---|
| | Unannounced Price Group | | Announced Price Group | | Unannounced Price Group | | Announced Price Group | |
| Interval | CAAR | t-stat. | CAAR | t-stat. | CAAR | t-stat. | CAAR | t-stat. |
| -12 through +12 | -0.1285 | -2.0726* | -0.2255 | -3.6371** | 0.0783 | 1.0951 | -0.2503 | -3.5007** |
| -12 through -1 | -0.1241 | -2.8928** | -0.0487 | -1.1352 | 0.0601 | 1.2141 | -0.0485 | -0.9798 |
| -12 through +6 | -0.0428 | -0.7911 | -0.1711 | -3.1627** | 0.0398 | 0.6388 | -0.1531 | -2.4575* |
| -6 through +6 | -0.0334 | -0.7472 | -0.2187 | -4.8926** | 0.0068 | 0.1318 | -0.0905 | -1.7539 |
| -1 through 0 | 0.0547 | 3.1257* | 0.0512 | 2.9257 | 0.0479 | 2.3713 | -0.0027 | -0.1337 |
| +2 through | -0.0811 | -1.9732* | -0.1220 | -2.9684** | -0.0264 | -0.5570 | -0.2089 | -4.4072** |
| +6 through + 12 | -0.0887 | -2.7043* | -0.1306 | -3.9817** | -0.0193 | -0.5106 | -0.1123 | -2.9709* |

* Significant at the 5% level.
** Significant at the 1% level.

average abnormal returns for the event month of the former group was 5.58 percent, while it was negative for the latter group—for month $-1$ it was 6.47 percent. The $t$-values for both the returns were significant at the 1 percent level.

When we examine the CAAR of the control firms for the same two groups, as shown in table 6.8, we find that here, too, the unannounced price group performed much better than the announced group with the disclosure of transaction prices. The CAAR of the entire twenty-five-month period for the former group was 7.83 percent, while for the announced price group it was $-25.03$ percent during the same period. But for the event months (i.e., months $-1$ and 0), the averge abnormal returns were also positive for the unannounced price group, while they were positive for the month prior to the event date for the announced price group, though not statistically significant. Apparently, public announcements of the transaction price disclosures worked negatively for the shareholders of these firms, both for the excellent and control samples.

In table 6.9, we have shown the CAAR for the unannounced and announced price groups of both the excellent and control firms over selected intervals. It is important to note that for the period of month $-12$ through month $-1$, the CAAR of the unannounced price group in the excellent sample was $-12.41$ percent, but for the same group in the control sample it was 6.01 percent. This was also true for the period of month $-12$ through month $+6$ for both the abovementioned groups. But for the event months, the CAAR of both the groups was positive, although it was slightly higher for the unannounced price group of the excellent sample. But in most of the time periods, the announced price group in both samples fared worse as compared to the unannounced price group. The disclosure of price in divestitures evidently acted as a negative signal to the investors of the selling firms.

## NOTES

1. K. Boudreaux, "Divestiture and Share Price," *Journal of Financial and Quantitative Analysis,*Vol. 10 (November 1975): 619–26.

2. G. Alexander et al., "Investigating the Valuation Effects of Announcements of Voluntary Corporate Selloffs," *Journal of Finance*, Vol. 39 (June 1984): 503–17.

3. P. C. Jain, "The Effect of Voluntary Sell-off Announcements on Shareholders' Wealth," *Journal of Finance,*Vol. 40 (March 1985): 209–24.

4. A. Klein, "The Timing and Substance of Divestiture Announcements: Individual, Simultaneous and Cumulative Effects," *Journal of Finance*, Vol. 41 (July 1986): 685–96.

5. E. Fama et al., "The Adjustment of Stock Prices for New Information," *International Economic Review*, Vol. 1 (Feb. 1969): 1–21.

6. M. Jensen and W. Meckling, "Theory of the Firm: Managerial Behavior, Agency Costs and Ownership Structure," *Journal of Financial Economics*, Vol 3 (October 1976): 305–60.

7. J. A. Miles and J. D. Rosenfeld, "The Effect of Voluntary Spin-off Announcements on Shareholder Wealth," *Journal of Finance*, Vol. 37 (Dec. 1983): 1597–1606.

8. A. Klein, "The Timing and Substance of Divestiture Announcements: Individual, Simultaneous and Cumulative Effects," pp. 693–94.

# 7

# Managerial Remuneration and Financial Performance of the Excellent and Control Firms, 1982–1986

The study of managerial remunerations and their relation to the performances of the companies concerned brings out the internal incentive structure of the firms, which includes the management of human resources in general and compensation policies in particular.[1] Current economic theory assumes the existence of reward systems that posit compensation so that a person's expected utility increases with observed productivity. The theory tends to focus on monetary rewards because individuals are willing to substitute nonmonetary for monetary rewards and because money represents a generalized claim on resources, and is therefore, in general, preferred over an equal dollar-value in kind.

Although many studies have found that pay is not very closely related to performance in many organizations, performance measurements and the attendant compensations are still important to evaluate a firm's overall performance.[2] This is particularly true in the case of the excellent companies, where higher compensations should be expected to go hand-in-hand with superior performance. Currently the restructuring of many firms emphasizes aligning managers' rewards more closely with the interests of shareholders, with emphasis on equity ownership, stock options, and annual bonus systems. But we have to realize at the same time that managers in hierarchical organizations are not principals in the sense usually modeled in the principal-agent literature.[3] Principals in such literature are 100 percent owners of the alienable residual claims to the cash flows, whereas in hierarchies, substitutes for residual claims are allocated to managers in the form of incentive contract and various direct-monitoring provisions.

Still, common to all theories is the overriding assumption that compensation must be tied to observed productivity.[4]

Any compensation analysis of firms must be divided into three parts—the *level*, the *functional form*, and the *composition*.[5] The level of compensation is the expected total cost of the pay package to the employer, or the expected total value of the pay package to the employee (i.e., the expected present value of the future stream of payoffs). It determines the quality and quantity of employees a firm can attract, which must be equal to the opportunity cost of the employees concerned. The *functional form* explains how the employees perform once they are hired—the relationship between pay and performance and the definition of performance. The *composition* of the pay package, on the other hand, defines the relative amounts of the components of the package, such as cash compensation, fringe benefits, quality of working environments, leisure, and so forth. It should be remembered, however, that when we discuss managerial remuneration, the discussion should be based on performance measured relative to the performance of all firms or firms in the same industry as we intend to do here, rather than on absolute measures of firm performance, as Holmström has so aptly pointed out.[6]

## THE LEVEL AND COMPOSITION OF MANAGERIAL REMUNERATION IN SELECTED EXCELLENT AND CONTROL FIRMS, 1982-1986

In tables 7.1 and 7.2, we have calculated the executive compensations of nineteen excellent and nineteen matching control firms, respectively, during the more recent period of 1982-1986. The data were culled from the proxy statements of the companies submitted to the Securities and Exchange Commission (SEC). The total compensations are divided into salary, bonus, and stock options, thus excluding the fringe benefits, savings plan, and annual accrued pension benefits. For stock options we have taken the net value realized in a given year (market value less exercise price) by an executive. For the calculation of executive compensations, we have used the monetary compensation of only the five top executives, namely, the chief executive (CEO), president (non-CEO), executive vice-president, senior vice-president, and the vice-president—all the persons whose compensations were *uniformly* provided in the proxy statements filed with the SEC. Although the SEC documents also contain the compensation of thirty-odd total executives as a group, the number varied from company to company, and therefore could not be used for our primary comparison. We

**Table 7.1**

**Executive Compensation of the Selected Excellent Firms, 1982–1986**

| Types of Executives | Compositions of Compensations | 1982 | | 1984 | | 1986 | |
|---|---|---|---|---|---|---|---|
| | | $ | % | $ | % | $ | % |
| Chief Exec. (CEO) | Salary | $14,366,690 | 60.72 | $15,831,971 | 68.63 | $17,726,584 | 64.61 |
| | Bonus | 1,826,522 | 7.72 | 1,260.336 | 5.46 | 1,283,000 | 4.68 |
| | Stock Options* | 7,466,582 | 31.56 | 5,975,848 | 25.91 | 8,424,924 | 30.71 |
| President (Non-CEO) | Salary | 9,681,680 | 73.38 | 10,656,646 | 66.02 | 10,995,215 | 68.92 |
| | Bonus | 1,189,337 | 9.01 | 965,476 | 5.98 | 838,000 | 5.25 |
| | Stock Options* | 2,323,040 | 17.61 | 4,518,848 | 28.00 | 4,120.563 | 25.83 |
| Exe. V P | Salary | 7,471.489 | 65.94 | 8,727,410 | 67.19 | 10,047,722 | 67.51 |
| | Bonus | 1,068,112 | 9.43 | 800,316 | 6.16 | 764,000 | 5.13 |
| | Stock Options* | 2,790,990 | 24.63 | 3,462,529 | 26.65 | 4,072,532 | 27.36 |
| Senior V P | Salary | 7,198,277 | 73.29 | 7,093,099 | 74.50 | 8,491,362 | 72.44 |
| | Bonus | 976,945 | 9.95 | 673,752 | 7.08 | 617,000 | 5.27 |
| | Stock Options* | 1,646,918 | 16.76 | 1,754,658 | 18.42 | 2,613,051 | 22.29 |
| V P | Salary | 6,537,917 | 71.01 | 6,902,262 | 76.18 | 8,083,542 | 56.91 |
| | Bonus | 769,160 | 8.35 | 608,673 | 6.72 | 550,000 | 3.87 |
| | Stock Options* | 1,900,188 | 20.64 | 1,548,944 | 17.10 | 5,569,419 | 39.22 |

*Net value realized (market value less exercise price).

Source: Proxy statements of the companies surveyed submitted to
the Securities and Exchange Commission, covering the
years 1982–1986.

**Table 7.2**

**Executive Compensation of the Selected Control Firms, 1982–1986**

| Types of Executives | Composition of Compensations | 1982 | | 1984 | | 1986 | |
|---|---|---|---|---|---|---|---|
| | | $ | % | $ | % | $ | % |
| Chief Exec. (CEO) | Salary | $13,048,397 | 57.70 | $14,379,471 | 69.84 | $15,769,698 | 68.93 |
| | Bonus | 2,271,814 | 10.05 | 2,610,693 | 12.68 | 2,587,327 | 11.31 |
| | Stock Options* | 7,292,627 | 32.35 | 3,599,690 | 17.48 | 4,521,144 | 19.76 |
| President (Non-CEO) | Salary | 9,183,675 | 53.10 | 10,051,130 | 75.08 | 11,372,352 | 67.36 |
| | Bonus | 1,660,911 | 9.60 | 1,766,848 | 13.20 | 2,173,726 | 12.88 |
| | Stock Options* | 6,449.139 | 37.30 | 1,569,985 | 11.72 | 3,335,778 | 19.76 |
| Exec. V-P | Salary | 7,005,001 | 59.86 | 7,805,893 | 66.78 | 8,371,640 | 61.79 |
| | Bonus | 858,671 | 7.34 | 1,221,702 | 10.44 | 1,491,056 | 11.01 |
| | Stock Options* | 3,839,247 | 32.80 | 2,679,298 | 22.88 | 3,684,938 | 27.20 |
| Senior V-P | Salary | 6,138,217 | 55.40 | 7,256,324 | 63.15 | 8,162,187 | 63.09 |
| | Bonus | 814,742 | 7.35 | 1,178,008 | 10.25 | 1,364,435 | 10.55 |
| | Stock Options* | 4,127,376 | 37.25 | 3,055,397 | 26.60 | 3,409,773 | 26.36 |
| V-P | Salary | 6,006,490 | 65.35 | 6,917,303 | 74.85 | 7,609,666 | 60.89 |
| | Bonus | 978,467 | 10.65 | 1,150,322 | 12.45 | 1,256,609 | 10.06 |
| | Stock Options* | 2,205,924 | 24.00 | 1,173,369 | 12.70 | 3,630,884 | 29.05 |

\* Net value realized (market value less exercise value).

Source: Proxy statements of the companies surveyed submitted to
the securities and Exchange Commission, covering the
years 1982-1986.

have, however, used the total executive compensation amount whenever our analysis for measuring firm performance called for it.

Table 7.1 shows that a large portion of the total compensations of the five top executives constituted stock options realized by these executives during the period covered by our study. Although the salaries alone, on average, made up about 60 percent of the total compensation of these executives in a given year, the percentage diminished if a substantial amount of stock options was realized in that year. Understandably, the realized values of stock options were generally scaled down in the hierarchical orders of the executives, although in 1986, the percentage of stock options realized was about 40 percent of the total compensation for vice-presidents among these selected excellent firms. The level of salary also diminished following the hierarchical ranks of the executives. Bonuses constituted a small portion of total compensation, no doubt because they are transitory in nature and provide little incentive for better performance, as was found by Murphy and others.[7]

When we compare, for 1982-1986, the compensation awarded to the top five executives in each of the nineteen excellent firms with the compensation awarded their counterparts among the control firms, as shown in table 7.2, we find that, generally, the latter group followed the same structure and characteristics as the excellent firms. Here, too, the net realized value of stock options constituted over 30 percent of total compensation to the top five executives in 1982, although the percentage declined subsequently for all ranks except vice-president. Bonuses shared less than 12 percent of total compensation in a given year for any of these executives. Also, the level of the salary component of the total compensation followed the same downward pattern of the hierarchical order. Interestingly, the level of salary in each rank was almost the same for these two groups of firms, thus indicating that the horizontal equity system is quite prevalent among U.S. business firms, particularly among the large firms. When we calculate the percentage change of total compensation for the top five executive positions in both the excellent and control firms during 1982-1986, as shown in table 7.3, we find that on average, the total compensation of the top five executives among the excellent firms increased over 25 percent in five years. The highest growth took place for the position of vice-president, followed by the executive vice-president, while the smallest growth occurred in the compensation of the chief executive officer (CEO). Since stock options comprised a large part of compensation, cashing them any time would naturally boost the total compensation of an executive. This happened in the case of the vice-presidents as a group during 1984-1986, when the net realized values of stock options during 1986 increased the total compensations of the vice-presidents by over 50 percent.

**Table 7.3**
**Percentage Change of Total Executive Compensation, 1982–1986**

| Types of Executives | Years | | |
|---|---|---|---|
| | 1982–1984 | 1984–1986 | 1982–1986 |
| A. Excellent Firms | | | |
| Chief Executive (CEO) | -2.50 | 18.93 | 15.95 |
| President (Non-CEO) | 22.35 | -1.16 | 20.93 |
| Exec. V-P | 14.66 | 14.57 | 31.36 |
| Senior V-P | -3.06 | 19.34 | 19.33 |
| V-P | -1.60 | 56.77 | 54.26 |
| Total | 5.32 | 18.95 | 25.28 |
| B. Control Firms | | | |
| Chief Executive (CEO) | -8.95 | 11.11 | 1.16 |
| President (Non-CEO) | -22.58 | 26.09 | -2.38 |
| Exec. V-P | 0.03 | 15.72 | 15.76 |
| Senior V-P | 3.69 | 12.59 | 16.75 |
| V-P | 0.55 | 35.97 | 35.98 |
| Total | -7.60 | 18.56 | 9.54 |

Source: Proxy statements of the companies surveyed submitted to the securities and Exchange Commission, covering the years 1982–1986.

We may note, however, that the compensation package of the chief executives as a group was less in 1986 than in 1984, which was also true for the senior vice-presidents as well as the vice-presidents. Similarly, the total compensation of the presidents as a group was slightly less in 1986 as compared to 1984.

As we examine the percentage change of total compensations for the top five executive positions of the control firms during 1982–1984, we find that although the total compensations increased by over 9 percent in five years, they were about two-thirds less than the total in the excellent firms during the same period. Compensation was again highest for the vice-presidents, due to the cashing of stock options during 1984–1986. Here, also, the growth of compensation for the CEOs was lowest during the period 1982–1986. However, the growth of compensation for the president was negative during this period, as it was for the CEOs and the

**Table 7.4**
**Executive Compensation of the Selected Excellent Firms, by Industry Groupings, 1982–1986**

| Industry Groupings | Years | | | | | |
|---|---|---|---|---|---|---|
| | 1982 | | 1984 | | 1986 | |
| | $ | % | $ | % | $ | % |
| **High Technology** | | | | | | |
| CEO | $3,591,318 | 24.44 | $6,998,369 | 37.13 | $6,146,207 | 38.81 |
| President | 3,374,492 | 22.98 | 3,910,962 | 20.75 | 2,685,646 | 16.96 |
| V-P | 7,722,650 | 52.58 | 7,938,901 | 42.12 | 7,005,003 | 44.23 |
| **Consumer Goods** | | | | | | |
| CEO | 5,294,134 | 35.24 | 5,015,394 | 32.40 | 6,833,429 | 34.62 |
| President | 2,668,792 | 17.76 | 3,702,360 | 23.91 | 3,810,452 | 19.30 |
| V-P | 7,059,992 | 47.00 | 6,763,718 | 43.69 | 9,097,295 | 46.08 |
| **General Industrial** | | | | | | |
| CEO | 1,840,356 | 30.64 | 2,466,974 | 23.44 | 2,489,726 | 28.30 |
| President | 1,351,054 | 22.50 | 2,375,923 | 22.58 | 1,829,761 | 20.80 |
| V-P | 2,814,619 | 46.86 | 5,680,168 | 53.98 | 4,478,922 | 50.90 |
| **Service** | | | | | | |
| CEO | 2,058,191 | 32.12 | 2,019,183 | 34.28 | 4,523,443 | 39.68 |
| President | 1,105,833 | 17.26 | 1,222,997 | 20.77 | 2,122,171 | 18.61 |
| V-P | 3,243,536 | 50.62 | 2,647,606 | 44.95 | 4,755,461 | 41.71 |
| **Project Mangement** | | | | | | |
| CEO | 5,109,974 | 52.14 | 1,638,267 | 28.17 | 1,587,242 | 27.96 |
| President | 1,511,686 | 15.43 | 1,004,144 | 17.27 | 926,779 | 16.32 |
| V-P | 3,178,373 | 32.43 | 3,173,084 | 54.56 | 3,163,742 | 55.72 |
| **Resource-Based** | | | | | | |
| CEO | 5,765,821 | 37.73 | 4,929,968 | 34.66 | 5,854,461 | 25.74 |
| President | 3,182,200 | 20.83 | 3,924,584 | 27.59 | 4,578,969 | 20.14 |
| V-P | 6,332,699 | 41.44 | 5,369,166 | 37.75 | 12,308,205 | 54.12 |

presidents during 1982–1984. For the control firms as well as the excellent firms, 1984–1986 was a better period than 1982–1984, when the bull market took a deeper hold and the values of stocks in these large, well-known companies started to soar.

In tables 7.4 and 7.5, we have divided the total compensations for the top five executives of both the excellent and control firms, respectively, for the period 1982–1986, into the six familiar industry groupings. For the top executive compensation of the excellent firms, as shown in table 7.4, the level of total compensations was highest in the resource-based sector, followed by the consumer goods sector, in both 1982 and 1986. The percentage share of the CEOs went up in the high technology and service sectors, while it went down slightly in the consumer goods and general industrial sectors, and only very slightly in the project management and resource-based sectors during 1982–1986. The main reason why executive compensations showed violent changes in project management was due to the fact that the sample was confined to two firms only, as noted before. As for the share of presidents' (non-CEOs) compensation, it went up slightly in the consumer goods, service, and project management sectors, but fell moderately in high technology, and slightly in the general industrial sectors during 1982–1986. Taking the compensations of three vice-presidents together, their share increased significantly both in project management and the resource-based sectors, while it fell moderately in the high technology and service sectors during this period. Again, the higher level of compensation of the CEOs in project management in 1982 was due to the cashing in of stock options.

As we examine the total compensations of the top five executives among the control firms during 1982–1986, we find that here, too, the total compensation was highest in the resource-based sector in 1982, but highest in the consumer goods sector in 1986. Also, the percentage of compensation for the CEOs as a group went up only in the consumer goods sector, while it went down significantly in the project management, service, and resource-based sectors in 1982–1986. The percentage share of the compensation for presidents as a group increased moderately in project management and slightly in the consumer goods sector, but went down in the remaining four industry groupings. The share of the three vice-presidents taken together increased slightly in the service, project management, and resource-based sectors, while declining moderately in the consumer goods sector during 1982–1986. But, in the majority of cases, the increase or decrease of compensation did not take place monotonically, as the figures in 1984 would attest.

**Table 7.5**

**Executive Compensation of the Selected Control Firms, by Industry Groupings, 1982–1986**

| Industry Groupings | Years | | | | | |
|---|---|---|---|---|---|---|
| | 1982 | | 1984 | | 1986 | |
| | $ | % | $ | % | $ | % |
| **High Technology** | | | | | | |
| CEO | $3,690,668 | 28.76 | $3,190,635 | 30.17 | $3,812,196 | 29.75 |
| President | 4,157,170 | 32.40 | 2,694,801 | 25.49 | 3,619,872 | 28.25 |
| V-P | 4,984,043 | 38.84 | 4,689,038 | 44.34 | 5,380,446 | 42.00 |
| **Consumer Goods** | | | | | | |
| CEO | 3,411,270 | 25.80 | 5,101,742 | 32.47 | 6,394,156 | 32.82 |
| President | 2,843,820 | 21.50 | 3,582,946 | 22.81 | 4,641,682 | 23.83 |
| V-P | 6,968,900 | 52.70 | 7,027,231 | 44.72 | 8,443,957 | 43.35 |
| **General Industrial** | | | | | | |
| CEO | 2,917,874 | 24.75 | 3,416,733 | 34.25 | 2,154,933 | 23.57 |
| President | 2,658,392 | 22.55 | 1,590,450 | 15.95 | 1,719,743 | 18.81 |
| V-P | 6,211,603 | 52.70 | 4,966,699 | 49.80 | 5,266,503 | 57.62 |
| **Service** | | | | | | |
| CEO | 3,670,019 | 37.14 | 3,422,642 | 30.07 | 3,439,703 | 30.82 |
| President | 1,948,247 | 19.72 | 1,703,318 | 14.96 | 1,231,641 | 11.04 |
| V-P | 4,262,677 | 43.14 | 6,256,259 | 54.97 | 6,487,944 | 58.14 |
| **Project Management** | | | | | | |
| CEO | 1,566,577 | 36.17 | 1,353,828 | 27.08 | 1,502,953 | 17.30 |
| President | 1,035,185 | 23.90 | 1,011,235 | 20.23 | 2,408,622 | 27.72 |
| V-P | 1,729,518 | 39.93 | 2,633,903 | 52.69 | 4,776,831 | 54.98 |
| **Resource-Based** | | | | | | |
| CEO | 7,356,430 | 37.11 | 4,104,273 | 29.80 | 5,574,228 | 31.93 |
| President | 4,650,911 | 23.46 | 2,804,213 | 20.36 | 3,260,276 | 18.67 |

When we look into percentage change of compensations for the top five executives, by groupings in 1982–1986, as shown in table 7.6, we find that among the excellent firms, the highest increase took place in the service sector, followed by the resource-based sector. The former was also highest during 1984–1986, but the general industrial sector was the highest during 1982–1984. For the whole period of 1982–1986, the only decline that took place was in project management, as was true in the two subperiods for·this sector. But in 1984, total executive compensations declined in the service and resource-based sectors when compared to 1982, while in 1986 the shares declined in the general industrial and high technology sectors as compared to 1984. Again, the majority of the groupings showed sharp fluctuation in percentage change during the two subperiods of our study.

**Table 7.6**
**Percentage Change of Executive Compensation, by Industry Groupings, 1982–1986**

| Industry Groupings | Years | | |
|---|---|---|---|
| | 1982–1984 | 1984–1986 | 1982–1986 |
| A. Excellent Firms | | | |
| High Tech. | 23.32 | -15.98 | 7.82 |
| Consumer Goods | 3.05 | 27.51 | 31.41 |
| General Indus. | 75.21 | -16.39 | 46.49 |
| Service | -8.08 | 93.57 | 77.93 |
| Project Manage. | -40.66 | -2.37 | -42.06 |
| Resource-Based | -6.92 | 59.89 | 48.83 |
| B. Control Firms | | | |
| High Tech. | 17.59 | 21.16 | -0.15 |
| Consumer Goods | 20.36 | 23.97 | 47.31 |
| General Indus. | -15.39 | -8.35 | -22.45 |
| Service | 15.19 | -1.96 | 12.94 |
| Project Manage. | 15.42 | 73.80 | 100.59 |
| Resource-Based | -30.33 | 26.77 | -11.93 |

Source: Proxy statements of the companies surveyed submitted to the securities and Exchange Commission, covering the years 1982–1986.

As for the percentage change of the total compensations for the top five executives of the control firms, we find that the highest positive change took place in project management during 1982–1986, although we must remember that the sample was confined to two firms only. Apart from that, only the consumer goods sector showed significant increase, while both the resource-based and high technology sectors showed a decline in top executive compensations during this period. In 1984, as compared to 1982, top executive compensations increased in the consumer goods, service, and project management sectors, while they declined in the high technology, general industrial, and resource-based sectors. Similarly in 1986, in comparison to 1984, the net percentage of total compensation increased in the project management, consumer goods, and high technology sectors, but declined moderately in the general industrial and only very slightly in the service sector. On average, the percentage increase of the total compensations for the top five executives of the control firms was only 9.54 percent, while it was 25.42 percent for the excellent firms during the entire half-decade of our study.

## MANAGERIAL REMUNERATION AND PERFORMANCE OF THE SELECTED EXCELLENT AND CONTROL FIRMS, 1982–1986

Many studies have found an apparent *lack* of correlation between managerial earnings and various measures of corporate performance, yet the level of executive compensation must be tied in with management's efforts to maximize the value of their firms.[8] Past studies generally have explored the issue of the relation of firm size (e.g., sales) to managerial remuneration, but other performance measures such as return on stockholders' equity, profits, or earnings per share should also be examined to determine their relationship to executive remuneration.[9] This is especially true for the excellent firms in which, after all, the increase in the management's total remuneration should be positively correlated with the growth of the stockholders' wealth.

In order to examine the relationship between managerial remuneration and the performance of both the excellent and control firms, we have calculated in table 7.7 the average annual compound growth of sales, assets, and net incomes, respectively, and compared them with the average annual compound growth of executive remuneration as a group during 1982–1986. Here we find that the average annual growth rate of executive compensation was higher than the average annual compound growth rate of sales in four of the six industry groupings, namely, the consumer goods, general industrial, service, and resource-based sectors. The average annual growth of managerial remuneration was higher than the average annual growth of assets in four out of six industry groupings also. Compared to the average annual compound growth of net incomes, the growth rate of executive compensation was higher in three of the six industry groupings. Surprisingly, the average annual growth of executive compensation was over 10 percent in the resource-based sector when the average growth rate of sales in that sector was negative, and the average annual growth rates of assets and net income was less than 3 percent during 1982–1986.

When we compare the average annual compound growth rate of executive compensation in the control firms to the growth of sales, assets, and net incomes, we find that the picture was almost the opposite of that in the excellent firms. Here, in three of the six industry groupings the growth rate of executive remunerations as a group was negative, while the average annual growth rates of sales and assets were positive. The growth rate of executive remuneration was less than the growth rate of sales in four

**Table 7.7**

**Managerial Remuneration and Performance of the Excellent and Control Firms, 1982–1986**

| Industry Groupings | Average Annual Compound Growth of Sales | Average Ann. Compound Growth of Assets | Ave. Ann. Compound Growth of Net Income | Ave. Ann. Compound Growth of Exe. Compen. |
|---|---|---|---|---|
| A. Excellent Firms | | | | |
| High Tech. | 6.17 | 9.34 | 6.82 | 1.90 |
| Consumer Goods | 6.73 | 12.71 | 4.04 | 7.07 |
| General Indus. | 9.56 | 5.98 | 7.76 | 10.02 |
| Service | 11.63 | 13.62 | 21.49 | 15.49 |
| Project Manage. | 3.52 | -2.08 | -21.64 | -12.76 |
| Resource-Based | -5.92 | 1.17 | 2.24 | 10.45 |
| B. Control Firms | | | | |
| High Tech. | 10.08 | 11.37 | 9.68 | -0.04 |
| Consumer Goods | 7.52 | 11.27 | 12.98 | 10.17 |
| General Indus. | 5.25 | 6.63 | -5.27 | -6.16 |
| Service | 7.69 | 11.17 | 5.89 | 3.09 |
| Project Manage. | 12.73 | 7.58 | 23.27 | 19.01 |
| Resource-Based | 1.52 | 8.87 | 10.40 | -3.13 |

Source: Proxy statements of the companies surveyed submitted to the securities and Exchange Commission, covering the years 1982–1986.

of the six groupings, while it was less than the annual growth rate of assets in five out of six industry groupings. When we compare the average annual growth of executive remuneration with the growth of net income, we find the startling fact that the rate of remuneration was lower than the rate of net income in *all* six industry groupings. Obviously, as far as pay-for-performance is concerned, the control firms did better than the excellent firms in all of the three performance criteria during the period covered by our study (i.e., 1982–1986).

In table 7.8 we have juxtaposed, again, the average annual compound growth rate of total executive compensation against the average annual compound growth rates of stock prices, earnings per share, and the return of stockholders' equity (percent return on net worth) for both the excellent and control firms during 1982–1986. Except in the high technology and

**Table 7.8**

**Managerial Remuneration and Stock Price Performance of the Excellent and Control Firms, 1982–1986**

| Industry Groupings | Average Annual Compound Growth of Price per Share | Average Annual Compound Growth of EPS | Average Annual Growth of % Earned on Net Worth | Average Annual Growth of Execu.Compen. |
|---|---|---|---|---|
| A. Excellent Firms | | | | |
| High Tech. | 16.95 | 2.97 | -7.74 | 1.90 |
| Consumer Goods | 17.65 | 3.92 | -2.79 | 7.07 |
| General Indus. | 8.38 | 18.40 | 8.61 | 10.02 |
| Service | 20.27 | 20.69 | 8.93 | 15.49 |
| Project Manage. | 13.32 | -7.46 | -3.50 | -12.76 |
| Resource-Based | 16.22 | 10.06 | 9.19 | 10.45 |
| B. Control Firms | | | | |
| High Tech. | 6.88 | 3.46 | -4.92 | -0.04 |
| Consumer Goods | 22.83 | 13.45 | 5.11 | 10.17 |
| General Indus. | 23.73 | -14.25 | -17.14 | -6.16 |
| Service | 14.67 | 7.41 | -0.32 | 3.09 |
| Project Manage. | 19.53 | 8.42 | -9.61 | 19.01 |
| Resource-Based | 13.34 | -0.67 | 7.59 | -3.13 |

Source: Value Line Investment Survey, covering the years 1982–1986, and the proxy statements of the companies, 1982–1986.

project management sectors, the growth rate of executive compensation among the excellent firms was higher than among control firms by at least one of these measures of firm performance. The growth rate of executive compensation was higher than the average annual growth rate of earnings per share in the consumer goods, service, and resource-based sectors, while significantly lower only in the general industrial and project management sectors during 1982–1986. During the same time period, the average annual growth rate of executive compensation was higher than the average annual growth rate of stockholders' equity in five of the six industry groupings. Only against the increase in stock prices was the growth rate of executive compensation lower for the majority of industry groupings covered by our study.

When we compare the growth rate of executive remuneration with these three measures of performance for the control firms, we find that here, again, the control firms did better on average than the excellent firms. Among all six industry groupings the average annual growth rate of

**Table 7.9**
**Executive Compensation as Percentage of Sales, Assets, and Net Income for Selected Excellent and Control Firms, 1982–1986**

| | Years | | |
|---|---|---|---|
| | 1982 | 1984 | 1986 |
| **A. Excellent Firms** | | | |
| Executive Comp. | | | |
| as % of Sales | 0.0919% | 0.0615% | 0.0630% |
| Executive Comp. | | | |
| as % of Assets | 0.1088 | 0.0870 | 0.0762 |
| Executive Comp. | | | |
| as % of Net Income | | | |
| Whole Exe. Group | 1.9457 | 1.1669 | 1.8918 |
| CEO | 0.1938 | 0.1293 | 0.2334 |
| Five Top Exe. | 0.5506 | 0.3966 | 0.7116 |
| **B. Control Firms** | | | |
| Executive Comp. | | | |
| as % of Sales | 0.0828% | 0.0635% | 0.0693% |
| Executive Comp. | | | |
| as % of Assets | 0.1031 | 0.0761 | 0.0752 |
| Executive Comp. | | | |
| as % of Net Income | | | |
| Whole Exe. Group | 2.7645 | 1.4216 | 1.4421 |
| CEO | 0.3834 | 0.1922 | 0.1866 |
| Five Top Exe. | 1.2189 | 0.6201 | 0.6421 |

Source: Proxy statements of the companies surveyed submitted to
the securities and Exchange Commission, covering the
years 1982–1986.

executive compensation was lower than the average annual growth rate of price per share, most often by a substantial margin. Except in the case of project management, the average annual growth of executive compensation was lower than the average annual growth of earnings per share in all industry groupings. The growth rate of executive compensation was not, however, that markedly superior when compared to the average annual growth rate of stockholders' equity. But here, too, the control firms did much better than the excellent firms, for the growth of executive compensation in the control group was higher than the growth of stockholders' equity in three of the six groupings, while in the excellent group, the growth of executive compensation was higher than that of stockholders' equity in five out of six industry groupings during 1982–1986.

In table 7.9 we have calculated the total executive compensation as percentage of sales, assets, and net incomes for both the selected excellent and control firms in 1982, 1984, and 1986, respectively. This table reveals that for the excellent firms, group executive compensation as a percentage of sales went down in 1984 and 1986 as compared to 1982. Executive compensation as a percentage of assets also went down in 1984 and further in 1986 as compared to 1982. But executive compensation as a percentage of net income dipped very little in 1986 as compared to 1982, while the compensation of the CEOs as percentage of net incomes actually went up moderately in 1986 as compared to 1982. This was also true for the compensation of the top five executives as percentage of net income. This increase was moderate from 1982 to 1986. But in all these three later groupings, there was a significant drop of the percentages from 1982 to 1984, followed by a sharp upturn in 1986.

In the selected control firms, executive compensation as percentage of sales also decreased from 1982 to 1986. The same was true for executive compensation as percentage of total assets of these firms during this period. But when it came to executive compensation as percentage of net incomes, the results were rather startling. The compensations of the whole executive group as percentage of net incomes went down by more than a full percentage point during these five years, while both the compensations of the CEOs as percentage of net incomes, and the compensations of the five top executives as percentage of net income declined significantly during the same period. This was exactly opposite of the result obtained for the excellent firms. Thus the managerial remunerations of the control firms were geared more to the firm performance than was the case for the excellent firms.

## RISKS, RETURNS, AND EXECUTIVE COMPENSATION IN THE EXCELLENT FIRMS

One of the basic tenets of modern finance theory is that the return of any asset must be commensurate with its underlying risk, (i.e., the higher the risk is, the higher the expected return should be). We all know now that a security (or asset) risk has two components—the unsystematic risk that can be diversified away, and the systematic or nondiversifiable risk, which is attributed to forces that affect all firms and are therefore not unique to any given firms. The Capital Asset Pricing Model (CAPM) as developed by Sharpe and others links together the relevant risk and return for all assets.[10] The way to measure systematic risk is to calculate the beta

**Table 7.10**

**Measures of Risk, Return, and Growth of Executive Compensation in the Selected Excellent Firms**

| Name of the Excellent Firms (By alphabetical order) | Mean Monthly Return(%) | Standard Deviation | Beta Coefficient | | Mean Growth of Total Exe. Compensation (%) |
|---|---|---|---|---|---|
| | | | CRSP | Value Line | |
| Atlantic Richfield | 1.595 | 7.597 | 0.51 | 0.85 | (-4.01) |
| Bristol-Myers | 1.207 | 7.230 | 0.69 | 0.95 | 1.86 |
| Caterpillar | 1.228 | 7.276 | 0.73 | 1.20 | -1.24 |
| Dana Corp. | 1.131 | 7.256 | 0.76 | 1.20 | -3.15 |
| Delta Airlines | 2.035 | 9.535 | 0.98 | 1.00 | 4.06 |
| Dow Chemical | 0.881 | 6.653 | 0.69 | 1.20 | 19.71 |
| Exxon | 1.151 | 5.040 | 0.41 | 0.80 | 1.17 |
| Fluor Corp. | 2.835 | 12.762 | 1.18 | 1.30 | -6.56 |
| General Electric | 0.683 | 6.553 | 0.70 | 1.10 | 1.53 |
| General Motors | 0.740 | 5.609 | 0.64 | 0.95 | 34.80 |
| Gould | 1.075 | 9.114 | 0.93 | 1.35 | 4.46 |
| Johnson & Johnson | 1.344 | 6.430 | 0.47 | 1.05 | 8.88 |
| K-Mart | 1.490 | 7.646 | 0.65 | 1.15 | 22.07 |
| Lockheed | 1.250 | 14.048 | 1.33 | 1.25 | -3.04 |
| Marriott | 1.292 | 11.726 | 1.09 | 1.10 | -6.61 |
| Merck | 1.149 | 6.601 | 0.45 | 0.90 | 18.53 |
| NCR | 0.960 | 9.147 | 0.99 | 1.25 | 0.99 |
| Procter & Gamble | 0.647 | 5.313 | 0.45 | 0.85 | 11.15 |
| TRW | 1.231 | 8.483 | 0.91 | 1.00 | -10.86 |

coefficient of an asset, which can be found by examining the asset's historic returns relative to the returns of the market. It is calculated by dividing the variance of returns for the market index into the covariance of returns of the $i^{th}$ asset with the market. One of the important uses of the beta coefficients is that they may be applied for ordinal rankings of the systematic risk of different assets.

In table 7.10, we have shown the mean monthly returns and the standard deviations of nineteen excellent firms, along with the beta coefficients of these stocks during the period 1961–1980—all calculated from the tapes of the Center for Research in Security Prices (CRSP) of the University of Chicago. In order to compare the changes of the beta coefficients from their historic value, we have also shown the beta values of these stocks as found in Value Line *Investment Survey*, which had calculated the beta coefficients for the period 1982–1986, a sixty-month period. Table 7.10 also gives the average annual growth rate of total executive compensation in these excellent firms during 1982–1986.

**Table 7.11**
**Ranking of Selected Excellent Firms by Risk, Return, and Mean Growth of Executive Compensation**

| Name of the Excellent Firms | Ranking by Mean Monthly Return (%) | Ranking by Value Line Beta Coefficient | Ranking by the Mean Growth Rate of Exe. Comp. |
|---|---|---|---|
| Atlantic Richfield | 3 | 17 | 16 |
| Bristol-Myers | 10 | 14 | 9 |
| Caterpillar | 9 | 5 | 13 |
| Dana Corp. | 13 | 6 | 15 |
| Delta Airlines | 2 | 12 | 8 |
| Dow Chemical | 16 | 7 | 3 |
| Exxon | 11 | 19 | 11 |
| Fluor Corp. | 1 | 2 | 17 |
| General Electric | 18 | 10 | 10 |
| General Motors | 17 | 15 | 1 |
| Gould | 14 | 1 | 7 |
| Johnson & Johnson | 5 | 11 | 6 |
| K-Mart | 4 | 8 | 2 |
| Lockheed | 7 | 3 | 14 |
| Marriott | 6 | 9 | 18 |
| Merck | 12 | 16 | 4 |
| NCR | 15 | 4 | 12 |
| Procter & Gamble | 19 | 18 | 5 |
| TRW | 8 | 13 | 19 |

This table reveals that in the real world the risk-return relationship is not that neat, that the companies that have the higher beta values do not necessarily reap the higher returns, although in some cases they come close to doing so. Companies such as Fluor had the highest monthly mean return, but also had the second-highest beta value during the period covered by our study. Similarly, Marriott had the third-highest beta value, but was number nineteen in terms of mean monthly return. Lockheed, however, which was number three in beta values, was number nine in mean monthly returns, and Dow Chemical, which was seven in beta value, was number sixteen in mean monthly returns during 1961-1980.

When we look into recent changes in the beta coefficients of these companies (as found in Value Line *Investment Survey*) and the recent growth of total executive compensations of these companies, we do not see any one-to-one correspondence with these two measures, which our theory would predict. For example, General Motors was number one in the growth

**Table 7.12**
**Frequency Distribution of the Difference Between the Average Monthly Returns of the Excellent and Control Firms**

| Year | Number of Times the Average Return for the Excellent Firms Exceeded the Control Firms* |
|------|:---:|
| 1961 | 8 |
| 1962 | 6 |
| 1963 | 7 |
| 1964 | 11 |
| 1965 | 7 |
| 1966 | 10 |
| 1967 | 7 |
| 1968 | 6 |
| 1969 | 11 |
| 1970 | 7 |
| 1971 | 8 |
| 1972 | 7 |
| 1973 | 8 |
| 1974 | 5 |
| 1975 | 8 |
| 1976 | 5 |
| 1977 | 5 |
| 1978 | 6 |
| 1979 | 2 |
| 1980 | 6 |

\* Because there are 12 months in a year, the maximum number is 12 and the minimum is 0.

Source: Basic data were collected from the monthly tapes of the Center for Research in Security Prices (CRSP), University of Chicago; see also W. Gary Simpson and Timothy Ireland, "Managerial Excellence and Shareholder Returns" (Working Paper), Oklahoma State University, Stillwater, Oklahoma, 1986.

of executive compensation in our sample, but was number fifteen in Value Line's beta values and number seventeen in mean monthly return. Similarly, Gould was number one in Value Line's beta values, but was number seven in the growth of executive compensation, and number fourteen in mean monthly return during 1961–1980. Even when we examine the changes in the beta values calculated from the CRSP data and the beta values calculated by Value Line for the same companies, we find anomalies between the theory (that the higher the beta value is, the higher the mean return and executive compensation as managerial reward should be) and reality. Dana Corporation's beta value jumped by forty-four points, but its executive compensation went down by 3.15 percent during the same period. The same was true for Caterpillar Tractor. General Electric's beta value increased by forty points but was tenth in the growth rate of executive compensations. Table 7.11 shows the ranking of these nineteen excellent firms in terms of mean monthly return, Values Line's beta values, and the growth rate of executive compensations. Nowhere do we find a close positive correlation among these three measures of risks, returns, and executive compensations.

Finally, we address the matter of mean returns again and compare them for the excellent firms and their competitors. As table 7.12 shows, in only twelve of the twenty years did the excellent firms clearly outperform the competitive firms in a twelve-month period in terms of mean monthly returns. Most of the superior returns of the excellent firms took place, however, in the earlier years of our study. If we take the mean monthly returns of the last ten years into account, we find that in only six years were the mean monthly returns of the excellent firms higher than those of the control firms on a twelve-month basis. If we take the last five years into account, then in no year did the excellent firms exceed the control firms in mean monthly returns within a year. Thus the deteriorating financial performance of the excellent firms in the later years of our study is confirmed again in this comparison of mean monthly returns.

## NOTES

1. G. Baker et al., "Compensations and Incentives: Theory vs. Practice," *Journal of Finance*, Vol. 43 (July 1988): 593–616.

2. E. Lawler III, *Pay and Organizational Effectiveness: A Psychological View* (New York: McGraw-Hill, 1971), pp. 117–39.

3. M. C. Jensen and W. Meckling, "Theory of the Firm: Managerial Behavior, Agency Costs and Ownership Structure," *Journal of Financial Economics*, Vol. 3 (Oct. 1976): 305–60.

4. K. J. Murphy, "Corporate Performance and Managerial Remuneration: An Empirical Analysis," *Journal of Accounting & Economics*, Vol. 7 (April 1985):11–42.

5. G. Baker et al., "Compensations and Incentives." p. 612.

6. B. Holmström, "Moral Hazard and Observability," *Bell Journal of Economics*, Vol. 10 (Spring 1979): 74–91.

7. K. Murphy, "Corporate Performance," pp. 26–29.

8. W. Lewellen and B. Huntsman, "Managerial Pay and Corporate Performance," *American Economic Review*, Vol. 60 (Sept. 1970): 710–20.

9. D. Ciscel and T. M. Carroll, "The Determinants of Executive Salaries: An Econometric Survey," *Review of Economic Statistics* Vol. 62 (Feb. 1980): 7–13.

10. William Sharpe, "Capital-Asset Prices: A Theory of Market Equilibrium under Condition of Risk," *Journal of Finance*, Vol. 19 (September 1964): 425–42.

# 8

# Summary and General Conclusions

## GENERAL SUMMARY OF THE FINDINGS

We have argued from the outset of our study that when we consider performance over a long period of time, there are no such things as excellent firms, because firms that are considered excellent at one point of time find it hard to maintain that position in the future. Again, if there is any above-normal return to the stockholders of those firms, it would be the result of undertaking abnormal risks, since return must be commensurate with risk in the long run. Moreover, so-called excellent firms must also go through the life cycle of the industries they belong to, and are therefore subject to relative decline as the industry moves toward maturity and stagnation. Finally, the excellent firms do not enjoy any long-term secure entrenchment by virtue of their size, capital, or management superiority, and like other firms are subject to the dynamics of market forces shaped by domestic competitive pressures, changes in consumer preferences, management turnover, and international competition. Therefore, by any measure, we will find that their performance will be uneven in the long run. In other words, the excellent firms will not remain so excellent when we examine their performance over a longer sweep of time, as we have done in our study of the United States' excellent firms listed in Peters and Waterman's book.

Since the growth of assets, sales, and earnings are the important yardsticks of a company's performance, they have been the starting point of our analysis. Here we find that the index of assets of the excellent firms grew remarkably well during the past twenty-five years covered by our study, since the index stood at 1,154.51 in 1984 when the base year was 1960 (i.e., 1960 = 100). But the comparable control firms from our sample did better than that, since the index of their assets stood at 1,234.04 (1960 = 100). Similarly, the average annual compound growth rate of assets of the excellent firms was 10.73 percent during 1960–1984, while the average annual compound growth rate of assets of the control firms was 11.04 percent for the same period. When we take the index and growth rate of sales of these two groups of firms, however, we find that the excellent firms did somewhat better than the control firms, since the index of sales of the former group stood at 1,298.41 in 1984 (1960 = 100), while the index of sales of the latter group reached 1,181.39 in 1984 (1960 = 100). The average annual compound growth rate of sales was also slightly higher among the excellent firms (11.27%) than among the control firms (10.84%).

As to the growth of earnings, aggregately the mean profit margin of the excellent firms for the twenty-five-year period was 6.01 percent, while for the control firms it was 4.77 percent. But for both the excellent and control firms, the net profit margin deteriorated during 1980–1984 as compared to 1975–1980. The decline was more severe for the excellent firms than the control firms; the profit margin fell for the excellent firms in five out of six industry groupings in the later time period. Again, if we exclude project management because of a very small sample size (only two firms), we find that the mean annual growth rate of earnings per share was slightly higher for the control firms (6.85%) than for the excellent firms (6.16%) for the period 1975–1984. When we rank the thirty leading firms of both the excellent and control groups by ten-year average growth of the earnings per share, we find the number of ranks in both these groups in a tie, thus indicating no overall superiority of the excellent firms in this regard.

As to the returns to stockholders' equity of the excellent and control firms, the mean return for the former group was 7.78 percent during 1960–1984, while the mean return for the latter group was 6.65 percent during the same period. It is important to note, however, that the growth rate as well as the return to investment deteriorated for both these groups during the later years (i.e., 1980–1984) of the study. The deterioration was more marked for the excellent firms. The return on investment fell in five out of six industry groupings among excellent firms, while among control firms it fell in only three out of six groupings during the latest period of our study.

We have also calculated the risk-adjusted returns of the excellent and control firms, following the Capital Asset Pricing Model (CAPM). To do this, we have used the mean returns, the Treynor measure, and the Sharpe measure for the three groups of firms that Peters and Waterman called "Top Performers," "Exemplar," and (ordinary) "Excellent," and we have compared these with the control firms and the market portfolio. Our analysis of risk and return confirms our earlier findings of a deterioration in the relative performance of the excellent firms over time. For the ten-year period (1960–1969), the excellent firm portfolio outperformed the market index and the control firm portfolio for five or more years, with but few exceptions. In the 1970–1979 period, however, relatively few measures indicate that the market or control firms were outperformed by the excellent firms. During 1980–1984, the excellent firms only outperformed the market for two years or less, according to all measures, although they generally outperformed the control firms in three of the five years. The Jensen measure also shows that for the last two subperiods (1975–1979 and 1980–1984), all but one excellent subsample have negative alphas, indicating inferior performance in later years.

Regarding the changes in financial ratios of both the excellent and control firms during 1960–1984, we find that for the excellent firms, the current ratio declined in all six industry groupings during the twenty-five years. The same trend of deterioration was also evident in all six industry groupings in the acid-test ratio and in the ratio of net working capital to total assets. In comparison to 1960, the latter ratio had fallen in all six industry groupings in 1984. This trend of declining ratios in later periods was also present among the control firms during the same period. Also, although the growth of cash flow for the excellent firms was slightly higher than for the control firms during 1975–1984, if we bar project management the average compound growth of cash flow was higher for the control firms than the excellent firms during this ten-year period.

As for the asset management or turnover ratios, the inventory-turnover ratio for the excellent firms increased from 1960 to 1984 in the general industrial and resource-based sectors, but went down in the remaining four industry groupings during the same period. The asset-turnover ratio of the excellent firms also went up in two groupings during 1960–1984. The fixed asset-turnover ratio of the excellent firms went down, however, in five of the six groupings from 1960 to 1984.

In contrast, the inventory-turnover ratio of the control firms increased from 1960 to 1984 in five of the six industry groupings. Also, the ratio went up in *all* groupings during 1980–1984—a situation markedly different from that of the excellent firms, where the ratio in three sectors deteriorated during the same period. The asset-turnover ratio of the control firms also improved in comparison to the excellent firms, as the ratio went up in three industry groupings while it went down in the remaining three groupings during 1960–1984. The same relatively improved situation for the control firms was observed in the case of the fixed asset-turnover ratio, where it went up in two industry groupings from 1960 to 1984. For the excellent firms, it increased in only one grouping during 1960–1984. Overall, the asset management of the control firms was better than the excellent firms during the last twenty-five years of our study. Altman's Z scores also confirmed the deteriorating situation of the excellent firms. Out of twenty-five excellent firms during 1975–1984, the Z score went down for fifteen companies, went up for eight firms, and remained virtually the same for the other two companies.

Regarding the measurement of operating efficiency of the excellent and control firms during 1975–1984, we find that although the average annual growth rate of gross plants and equipment for the excellent firms was higher than for the control firms, the overall growth rate of the gross plants and equipment of the excellent group fell by 13 percent from 1975 to 1984. Also, the operating ratio of the excellent firms on average went down more than that of the control firms during this period. As far as sales per employee are concerned, they were much higher among the control firms in the high technology, consumer goods, and general industrial sectors in both 1975 and 1984, but higher in the project management and resource-based sectors of the excellent firms in both 1975 and 1984. In the measurement of net income per employee, however, the excellent firms were superior to the control firms in all six industry groupings, both in 1975 and 1984.

In our calculation for the sales per dollar of gross plants and equipment of these two groups of firms during 1975–1984, the control firms on average did slightly better than the excellent firms. They also did better when we compare the net income per dollar of gross plants and equipment during 1975–1984. When we rank the 36 publicly held excellent firms in our total sample of 108 firms by the four measures of operating efficiency, we find that only 13 of these excellent firms ranked within the top 36 firms in terms of sales per employee, and 15 excellent firms ranked within the top 36 firms in terms of net income per employee. In the ranking of firms in terms of sales per dollar of gross plants and equipment, the number of excellent firms among the top 36 was 16, but the situation became worse again in the ranking by per dollar of gross plants and equipment, when only 6 excellent firms were included among the top 36 firms. Nowhere did the excellent firms form a majority in these rankings of operating efficiency.

When we test the optimal capital structure of these two groups of firms during 1975–1984, we find that the excellent firms did somewhat better than the control firms when we examine the ratio of long-term debt to total assets. According to optimal capital structure theory this ratio should decline over time. Among the excellent firms it did, in fact, go down in four of the six industry groupings, while for the control firms, the ratio went down clearly in three of the six groupings during 1975–1984. The situation was, however, the reverse with respect to the ratio of long-term debt to net worth. Here the control firms on average slightly outperformed the excellent firms. When we compare the ratio of long-term debt to total capital, the excellent firms as a whole performed relatively better, as the ratio fell in five of the six industry groupings during 1975–1984, while it fell in four of the six groupings among the control firms during the same period. The excellent firms also did better by the measure of the ratio of total liabilities to net worth, as the ratio fell in four of the six groupings among the excellent firms, but went down in only two of the six groupings among the control firms during 1975–1984.

According to the optimal capital structure theory, the ratio of net worth to total assets as well as the ratio of cash flow to long-term debt should be increasing over time. Among the excellent firms the ratio of net worth to total assets did go up in four out of the six industry groupings in 1984 as compared to 1975. Among the control firms, however, it also went up in four out of six groupings during the same period. But on average, the ratio of net worth to total capital increased by 12.66 percent for the control firms in 1975–1984, while for the excellent firms it increased by only 5.45 percent during the same period. As for the ratio of cash flow to long-term debt for both the groups during 1975–1984, the ratio for the excellent firms grew in two groupings but fell in three groupings during 1975–1984, while it increased more clearly in three of the six industry groupings among the control firms and fell in only two groupings over the same period. Although this ratio deteriorated in the majority of groupings in both samples of firms during 1980–1984 as compared to 1975–1980, the decline was much more pronounced for the excellent firms than the control firms.

Using the event study methodology as developed in finance literature over the past twenty years, we have tried to determine the returns to the stockholders from the acquisition of other corporations by both the excellent and control firms during 1960–1984. Our study has found that the cumulative average abnormal returns (CAAR) earned by the excellent firms for the twenty-five-month observation period were slightly higher than the CAAR obtained by the control firms during the same period. But when we compare the CAAR for the twelve-month period prior to the event month—the period that counts most in event studies—we find that the control firms performed better than the excellent firms, which was also true from month $-12$ through month $+6$. Even in the case of the CAAR for months immediately before the announcement of mergers, the control firms did slightly better than the excellent firms.

As to the impact on the abnormal returns of larger versus smaller acquisitions by these firms, we find that for the excellent group, firms with larger acquisitions had much higher CAAR as compared to the firms with smaller acquisitions. But this was not true for the selected control group firms, where the firms with smaller acquisitions had a superior CAAR. The result is the same when we compare the CAAR of the $-12$ month period prior to the event month for these two groups of firms. Thus the favorable scale effects due to larger size worked better for the excellent firms, while for the control firms, better negotiation and superior management of smaller acquisitions led them to a much higher cumulative return.

When we divide the complete sample into the two subsamples of larger and smaller divestitures, the results are mixed. The CAAR of the excellent firms that had gone through larger divestiture was $-12.95$ percent for the twenty-five-month period, and it was $-17.28$ percent for firms with smaller divestitures belonging to the same group for the same period. But for the control firms, the CAAR of firms with smaller divestitures was $-5.13$ percent, while it was $-20.56$ percent for firms with larger divestitures during the entire observation period. Interestingly, the average abnormal returns were positive, for both the excellent and control firms with larger divestiture, for the month before the announcement, but they were negative for firms with smaller divestitures for both the excellent and control firms.

As for the effects of disclosure versus non-disclosure of the transaction prices for these divestitures, the CAAR of the entire observation period was better in the case of non-price disclosure for both the excellent and control firms. Here again, the control firms performed much better than the excellent firms, although for divestitures with transaction price disclosure the CAAR figures were significantly negative for both groups. In all, the performances of the control firms were better than the excellent firms in the complete sample, and also in the subsample of divestitures with transaction price disclosures. Obviously, the excellent firms did not enjoy any superior performance from voluntary divestitures, as far as the returns to the stockholders were concerned.

When we compare the abnormal returns of firms with conglomerate acquisitions to those firms with non-conglomerate acquisitions, we find that here, too, the results are mixed. For the excellent group, on one hand, the CAAR of firms with non-conglomerate acquisitions was much higher than that of conglomerate acquisitions. For the control group, on the other hand, the CAAR of firms with conglomerate acquisitions was higher than the non-conglomerate acquisitions, although the difference was slight. Obviously, the perceived benefits of synergy for conglomerate acquisitions did not work for the excellent firms, but for the control firms the benefits accrued from conglomeration were also very modest during the twenty-five-month observation period.

Regarding the returns to the stockholders from the divestitures by these two groups of firms during 1960–1984, we have found that both the excellent and control firms of our sample earned a small positive abnormal return around the time of announcement of the divestiture, as has been found in other similar studies, although both groups had negative average abnormal returns when the entire twenty-five-month observation period was taken into account. Here, however, the control firms performed better than the excellent firms, as the CAAR of the former group was $-10.82$ percent, while the CAAR of the latter group was $-17.25$ percent during the twenty-five-month observation period. Also, for the time interval of $+12$ month through 0 month, the CAAR of the excellent firms was $-6.52$ percent, while for the control firms it was only $-0.10$ percent. Thus the performance of the control firms was better than the excellent firms for both these important time periods in the event studies.

As for the managerial remunerations and financial performances of the selected excellent and control firms during the more recent years of 1982–1986, we found that generally both groups had followed the same structure and characteristics, as net realized value of stock options constituted a very large part of total remunerations while bonuses were a small part of the package. When we calculate the percentage change of total compensation for the top five executive positions, we find that among the excellent firms they had increased over twenty-five percent in five years, while among the control firms they had increased by about two-thirds less than that. As for the correlation between the growth of executive compensation and growth of assets, sales, and net income, we find that for the excellent firms, the average annual growth rate of executive compensations was higher than either the average annual growth of sales or assets in four out of six industry groupings; but among the control firms the reverse was true, and the average annual growth of executive compensation was lower than the average annual growth of net income in *all* six groupings. Also, against the average growth rate of price per share as well as the earnings per share, the growth rate of executive compensation of the control firms was less than that of the excellent firms.

Regarding the relationship among risks, returns, and executive compensation in the selected excellent firms, we detect that the companies that had the higher beta values did not necessarily enjoy higher returns, nor did they have the highest growth of executive compensations. In very few cases did we find any close relationship among the measures of risks, returns, and executive compensations. Obviously, the management of the excellent firms did not perform that well in the risk-return world they faced.

## RECENT PERFORMANCE OF THE EXCELLENT FIRMS (1984–1986)

We have seen that the majority of the excellent firms did not perform as well as might be expected during the twenty-five years (1960–1984) covered by our study. In many performance measures they performed worse than the comparative control firms when both were taken as groups. In assets or earnings growth, risk-adjusted returns, returns to stockholders' equity, operating efficiency, and performance-based managerial remunerations, the excellent firms could not claim to be excellent during the long sweep of time we have studied here. They did perform better than their competitors in some particular subperiods, or in some industry groupings. But taken in their entirety, the United States' excellent firms could not maintain their lofty position for long. Instead, being subject to the same pressures and cycles as other firms, they performed quite normally, and momentary excellence regressed toward the norm over time.

Much more important is the fact that the financial performance of the excellent firms deteriorated considerably during the last years of our study. As Michelle Clayman discovered, the majority of the excellent companies began to deteriorate virtually from the date on which they were selected as excellent.[1] Even the most recent study of Kolodny et al. on the management performance of the excellent firms found no statistically significant difference in investment performance either as compared to the average NYSE-listed firm or to a control sample of firms with similar attributes.[2] In comparison to the relatively few statistically significant exceptions detected, the number of instances of inferior performance equaled or exceeded the number of cases of superior performance.

**Table 8.1**
**Net Profits, Earnings per Share, and Returns to Stockholders' Equity for 32**
**Excellent U.S. Firms, 1984–1986**

| Name of the Excellent Firm | Net Profits (%) | | Earnings per Share ($) | | Returns to Stockholders' Equity (%) | |
|---|---|---|---|---|---|---|
| | 1984 | 1986 | 1984 | 1986 | 1984 | 1986 |
| Amdahl | 3.8 | 4.17 | 0.64 | 0.81 | 6.9 | 7.9 |
| Avon | 5.8 | 5.5 | 2.16 | 2.23 | 15.7 | 23.3 |
| Boeing | 3.8 | 4.1 | 2.67 | 4.28 | 10.6 | 13.8 |
| Bristol-Myers | 11.3 | 12.6 | 1.73 | 2.14 | 22.0 | 21.5 |
| Caterpillar | NMF* | 2.4 | (2.60) | 1.80 | NMF* | 5.7 |
| Dana Corp. | 5.4 | 3.2 | 3.52 | 2.30 | 15.6 | 12.3 |
| Data General | 5.8 | 1.0 | 2.6 | 0.46 | 4.6 | 1.8 |
| Delta Airlines | 4.1 | 1.0 | 4.42 | 1.18 | 16.7 | 3.6 |
| Digital Equipment | 5.9 | 8.1 | 2.87 | 4.81 | 8.3 | 10.8 |
| Disney Productions | 6.5 | 10.0 | 0.75 | 1.82 | 9.3 | 17.4 |
| Dow Chemical | 4.5 | 6.7 | 2.50 | 3.87 | 9.6 | 14.3 |
| Du Pont | 4.0 | 5.7 | 5.89 | 6.35 | 11.6 | 11.5 |
| Eastman Kodak | 8.7 | 3.2 | 2.54 | 1.11 | 12.9 | 5.9 |
| Flour Corp. | NMF* | NMF* | 0.01 | (0.35) | 1.0 | NMF* |
| Hewlett-Packard | 9.1 | 7.3 | 2.13 | 2.02 | 15.4 | 11.8 |
| Intel | 11.0 | NMF* | 1.02 | (1.57) | 13.2 | NMF* |
| IBM | 14.3 | 9.3 | 10.77 | 7.81 | 24.9 | 13.9 |
| Johnson & Johnson | 8.4 | 4.7 | 2.75 | 1.85 | 16.7 | 11.1 |
| K-Mart | 2.4 | 2.4 | 2.56 | 2.84 | 15.4 | 14.5 |
| Marriott | 3.8 | 3.6 | 1.0 | 1.40 | 20.0 | 19.3 |
| Maytag | 9.8 | 7.6 | 1.16 | 1.51 | 27.6 | 23.6 |
| McDonald's | 11.4 | 11.3 | 1.95 | 2.49 | 19.4 | 19.1 |
| Merck | 13.9 | 16.4 | 1.12 | 1.62 | 19.4 | 26.3 |
| Minnesota Mining | 9.5 | 9.1 | 3.14 | 3.40 | 19.2 | 17.5 |
| National Semiconductor | 3.4 | NMF* | 0.66 | (1.73) | 9.1 | NMF* |
| Procter & Gamble | 6.6 | 4.6 | 5.17 | 4.20 | 16.9 | 11.9 |
| Raychem | 4.7 | 6.1 | 1.02 | 1.55 | 9.2 | 10.8 |
| Schlumberger | 19.8 | NMF* | 4.10 | (5.76) | 16.9 | NMF* |
| Standard Oil (Ind.)/Amoco | 7.9 | 5.1 | 7.51 | 3.60 | 17.1 | 8.2 |
| Texas Instruments | 5.4 | 0.8 | 4.24 | 0.38 | 20.0 | 2.3 |
| Wal-Mart | 4.2 | 3.8 | 0.48 | 0.80 | 27.3 | 26.6 |
| Wang Laboratories | 9.6 | 1.9 | 1.51 | 0.35 | 16.8 | 3.5 |

NMF* = Not meaningful due to losses in the initial terminal
        year of the study.

Source: Value Line _Investment Survey_, 1987.

In table 8.1, we display data on the latest financial performance of the thirty-two excellent firms taken from the Value Line *Investment Survey*.[3] These thirty-two excellent firms belong to Peters and Waterman's list of thirty-six publicly held excellent firms that were truly excellent (i.e., which met all their tests of excellence). Almost all of them performed poorly in 1986 when compared with their performances in 1984. In the three financial performance measures we have taken here—net profits, earnings per share, and returns to stockholders' equity (percentage of returns on net worth)—only eight (25 percent) of the total firms in our sample improved their performances in all three measures during 1984–1986. Fifteen (47 percent) of the firms deteriorated in all three areas, and 9 percent firms improved in one or two measures but fell off in the third one. In net profits, the performance of twenty-two, or about 69 percent of the total firms deteriorated from 1984 to 1986. In earnings per share, fifteen firms, or 46 percent of the total, declined from 1984 to 1986. And in the all-important measure of returns to stockholders' equity, twenty-one, or over 68 percent, of the total firms showed lower returns in 1986 as compared to 1984.

Thus our conclusion regarding the deteriorating financial positions of the excellent firms as a group in later years is fully supported by the statistics compiled by Value Line *Investment Survey* when we extend the study to include 1984–1986. Many of the so-called excellent firms have fallen into hard times because of domestic competitive pressures, changes in consumer preference (particularly for imported goods), higher leverages to finance mergers and acquisitions and other restructurings, and the impact of international competition on the U.S. markets. These factors will equally affect their performance in years to come. Since they were not excellent as a group in terms of many financial measures in the past, it is doubtful whether they will attain the right to be called excellent again in the foreseeable future.

## NOTES

1. Michelle Clayman, "In Search of Excellence—The Investor's Viewpoint," *Financial Analysts' Journal*, Vol. 43 (May/June 1987): 54–63.

2. Richard Kolodny et al., "In Search of Excellence . . . for Whom?" *Journal of Portfolio Management*, Vol. 15 (Spring 1989): 56–60.

3. Value Line *Investment Survey*, 1987 Edition.

# Appendix A
# Acquisitions by the Selected Excellent Firms, 1960–1984

| Acquiring Firm | Acquired Firm | Date of Announcement |
|---|---|---|
| | High Technology | |
| Emerson Electric | Skil Corp. | Jan. 3, 1979 |
| Hewlett-Packard | Field Emission Corp. | May 17, 1973 |
| NCR | Combined Paper Mills | April 25, 1969 |
| Schlumberger | Daystrom, Inc. | Aug. 24, 1961 |
| United Technologies | Otis Elevator | Oct. 16, 1975 |
| Xerox | Crum & Forster | Sept. 22, 1982 |
| General Electric | Utah International | March 16, 1976 |
| | Consumer Goods | |
| Eastman Kodak | Atex, Inc. | Oct. 10, 1981 |
| General Foods | Oscar Meyers, Inc. | Feb. 2, 1981 |
| Johnson & Johnson | Graham Mfg. Co. | Oct. 7, 1970 |
| Procter & Gamble | A. Folger & Co. | Aug. 30, 1963 |
| Avon | Tiffany & Co. | Nov. 22, 1978 |
| Bristol-Myers | Drackett Co. | March 22, 1965 |
| Chesebrough-Pond's | Ragu Packing Co. | Nov. 18, 1969 |
| Levi Strauss | Koracorp. Industries | March 21, 1979 |
| Maytag | Hardwick Store Co. | July 11, 1980 |
| Merck | Baltimore Aircoil Co. | Feb. 17, 1970 |
| | General Industrial | |
| Ingersoll-Rand | Torrington Co. | Oct. 11, 1968 |
| Minnesota Mining | Dynacolor Corp. | April 4, 1963 |
| | Service | |
| Delta Airlines | Northeast Airlines | Jan. 20, 1971 |
| American Airlines | Trans-Caribbean Airline | Jan. 19, 1970 |
| Wal-Mart | Kuhn Big-K Store | Jan. 23, 1981 |
| | Project Management | |
| Boeing | Vertol Aircraft Co, | Jan. 19, 1960 |
| Fluor Corp. | Daniel International | April 29, 1976 |
| | Resource-Based | |
| Exxon | Reliance Electric Co. | May 21, 1979 |
| Arco | Sinclair Oil | Nov. 1, 1968 |
| Dow Chemical | Allied Laboratories | Aug. 31, 1960 |
| DuPont | Remington Arms | Nov. 20, 1979 |
| Standard Oil (Ind.)/Amoco | Midwest Oil Co. | July 22, 1971 |

# Appendix B
# Acquisitions by the Selected Control Firms, 1960–1984

| Acquiring Firm | Acquired Firm | Date of Announcement |
|---|---|---|
| | High Technology | |
| Fairchild Industries | Republic Aviation Corp. | July 9, 1965 |
| Foxboro Corp. | Trans-Sonics, Inc. | March 6, 1974 |
| Harris Corp. | Radiation, Inc. | April 3, 1967 |
| Tandy Corp. | Radio Shack Corp. | April 3, 1963 |
| Raytheon | Iowa Mfg. Co. | Dec. 13, 1971 |
| Johnson Controls | Globe-Union, Inc. | May 30, 1978 |
| Motorola | Universal Data Systems | Nov. 10, 1978 |
| Zenith | The Health Co. | July 17, 1979 |
| | Consumer Goods | |
| Coca-Cola | Minute Maid Corp. | Sept. 9, 1960 |
| Colgate-Palmolive | Kendall Co. | May 17, 1972 |
| American Brands | Sunshine Biscuits, Inc. | Jan. 14, 1966 |
| Kellogg | Fern International | July 21, 1970 |
| Kroger Co. | Dillon Companies, Inc. | Nov. 16, 1982 |
| American Home Product | Corometrics Medical Syst. | Sept. 27, 1974 |
| Philip Morris | Mission Viejo | Oct. 2, 1972 |
| Warner-Lambert | American Chicle Co. | July 25, 1962 |
| Pfizer | Howmedica, Inc. | July 25, 1972 |
| | General Industrial | |
| Borg-Warner | Baker Industries, Inc. | Nov. 8, 1977 |
| Cabot Corp. | Kawecki Berylco Indus. | March 21, 1978 |
| | Service | |
| United Airlines | Wester Inter. Hotel | March 20, 1970 |
| J.C. Penney | Educator & Executive Co, | Feb.6, 1973 |
| Federated Dept. Stores | Rich's Inc. | July 12, 1976 |
| Walgreen | Rennebohm Drug Store | July 10, 1979 |
| | Project Management | |
| Grumman | Flexible Co. | Sept. 19, 1977 |
| Martin Marietta | Wedron Silica Co. | June 29, 1979 |
| | Resource-Based | |
| Standard Oil of Calif. | Mt. Diablo Co. | April 4, 1964 |
| Occidental Petroleum | Cities Service Co. | Aug. 16, 1982 |
| Allied Corp. | Union Texas Nat. Gas Co. | Nov. 21, 1961 |
| Monsanto | Fisher Governor Co. | Feb. 25, 1969 |

# Appendix C
# Divestiture by the Selected Excellent Firms, 1960–1984

| Divesting Firm | Divested Division | Date of Announcement |
|---|---|---|
| **High Technology** | | |
| Gould | Electrostatic Printer/ Plotter Product Line | July 16, 1979 |
| IBM | Service Bureau Corp. | Jan. 16, 1973 |
| NCR | Appleton Paper Division | May 8, 1978 |
| Rockwell | Admiral Domestic Appliance | Jan. 30, 1979 |
| Westinghouse | Domestic Major Appliance Business | Dec. 30, 1974 |
| Xerox | WUI | June 16, 1982 |
| Lockheed | Hollywood-Burbank Airport | April 3, 1978 |
| TRW | IRC Potentiometer | April 14, 1977 |
| **Consumer Goods** | | |
| Procter & Gamble | Commercial Laundry Supplies Division | Oct. 5, 1983 |
| Merck | Calgon Consumer Products | March 3, 1977 |
| Blue Bell | Salant Plants | Nov. 18, 1976 |
| General Foods | Berger Chef Systems | Dec. 10, 1981 |
| **General Industrial** | | |
| McDermott | Control Components International Division | July 14, 1981 |
| General Motors | Frigidaire Appliance Div. | Feb. 1, 1979 |
| **Service** | | |
| Marriott | Rustler Steak House Restaurants | Jan. 13, 1983 |
| Disney Productions | Celebrity Sports Center | April 3, 1979 |
| **Project Management** | | |
| Boeing | unit of Boeing Commerical Airplane Co. | Jan. 8, 1981 |
| Fluor Corp. | most of foreign oil & gas holdings | Dec. 19, 1983 |
| **Resource-Based** | | |
| Arco | 50% interest in American Chemical Co. | Oct. 9, 1974 |
| Dow Chemical | sold gas, oil wells, and leasehold acres | Jan. 7, 1977 |
| DuPont | News-Journal Co. | Jan. 31, 1978 |
| Standard Oil (Ind.)/ Amoco | Cyprus Anvil Mining Co. (majority interests) | Aug. 10, 1981 |

## Appendix D
## Divestiture by the Selected Control Firms, 1960–1984

| Divesting Firm | Divested Division | Date of Announcement |
|---|---|---|
| | High Technology | |
| Bell & Howell | Data-tape Division | Aug. 11, 1983 |
| Cabot Corp. | Machinery Division | July 2, 1980 |
| Harris Corp. | Printing-equipment Business | Dec. 9, 1982 |
| Motorola | Home-receiver Business | March 13, 1974 |
| Northop Corp. | Northrop Architectural Systems | Aug. 5, 1982 |
| Tandy Corp. | Allied Electronics Division | March 13, 1978 |
| Zenith | Hearing Instrument Business | Oct.. 11, 1977 |
| Fairchild Industries | sold entire interests of Banker Ramo Corp. | June 17, 1981 |
| | Consumer Goods | |
| Coca-Cola | Wine Business | Sept. 27, 1983 |
| Kroger Co. | Top Value Enterprises, Inc. | Dec. 11, 1978 |
| American Brands | Duffy-Mott Co. | Feb. 17, 1982 |
| General Mills | Toms Food Div. | April 19, 1983 |
| | General Industrial | |
| Borg-Warner | Morse Industrial Unit | Jan. 17, 1983 |
| Sears | Warwick Electronics (majority interests) | Aug. 11, 1966 |
| | Service | |
| Federated Dept. Stores | real-estate properties | Oct. 7, 1983 |
| J. C. Penney | Great American Reserve Insurance Company | June 21, 1983 |
| | Project Management | |
| Grumman | Grumman Flexible Co. | May 17, 1983 |
| | Resource-Based | |
| Mobil | sold its farm fertilizer business | Nov. 4, 1969 |
| Monsanto | Lion Oil Refining | July 7, 1972 |

# Selected Bibliography

## BOOKS

Altman, E. *Financial Distress*. New York: John Wiley & Sons, 1983.

Amling, F. *Investments*. Englewood Cliffs, N.J.: Prentice-Hall, 5th edition 1984.

Brealey, M., and Myers, S. *Principles of Corporate Finance*. New York: McGraw-Hill, 1981.

Brigham, E. *Fundamentals of Financial Management*. Hinsdale, Ill.: The Dryden Press, 5th edition 1989.

Kaplan, A. D. H. *Big Enterprise in a Competitive System*. Washington, D.C.: The Brookings Institute, rev. ed. 1964.

Lawler III, E. *Pay and Organizational Effectiveness: A Psychological View*. New York: McGraw-Hill, 1971.

Peters, T. J., and Waterman, R. H. *In Search of Excellence: Lessons from America's Best Run Companies*. New York: Harper & Row, 1982.

Reilly, F. K. *Investment Analysis and Portfolio Management*. Hinsdale, Ill.: The Dryden Press, 2nd edition 1985.

Servan-Schreiber, J.-J. *The American Challenge*. Atheneum, 1968.

## ARTICLES

Alexander, G., Benson, G., and Kampmeyer, J. "Investigating the Valuation Effects of Announcement of Voluntary Divestitures." *Journal of Finance*, Vol. 39 (June 1984): 503–17.

Asquith, P., and Kim, E. H. "The Impact of Merger Bids on the Participating Firms' Security Holders." *Journal of Finance*, Vol. 37 (Dec. 1982): 1209–28.

Baker, G., Jensen, M., and Murphy, K. J. "Compensations and Incentives: Theory vs. Practice." *Journal of Finance,* Vol. 43 (July 1988): 593–616.

Bradley, M., Jarrell, G., and Kim, E. "On the Existence of an Optimal Capital Structure: Theory and Evidence." *Journal of Finance,* Vol. 39 (July 1984): 857–78.

Brown, S., and Warner, J. "Measuring Security Price Performance." *Journal of Financial Economics,* Vol. 8 (September 1980): 205–58.

Castanias, R. "Bankruptcy Risk and Optimal Capital Structure." *Journal of Finance,* Vol. 38 (Dec. 1983): 1617–35.

Carroll, D. T. "A Disappointing Search for Excellence." *Harvard Business Review,* Vol. 61 (Dec. 1983): 78–88.

Cleyman, M. "In Search of Excellence—The Investor's Viewpoint." *Financial Analysts' Journal,* Vol. 43 (May-June 1987): 54–63.

DeAngello, H., and Masulis, R. "Optimal Capital Structure under Corporate and Personal Taxation." *Journal of Financial Economics,* Vol. 8 (March 1980): 3–29.

Dodd, P. R., and Ruback, R. "Tender Offers and Stockholders' Returns: An Empirical Analysis." *Journal of Financial Economics,* Vol. 5 (December 1977): 351–74.

Fama, E., Fisher, L., Tensen, M., and Roll, R. "The Adjustment of Stock Prices for New Information." *International Economic Review,* Vol. 1 (Feb. 1969): 1–21.

Ghosh, Arabinda. "Corporate Acquisitions and Stockholders' Returns in the United States' Excellent Firms." *North American Review of Economics and Finance,* Vol. 1 (December 1988): 101–29.

Halpern, P. "Empirical Estimates of the Amount and Distribution of Gains to Companies in Mergers." *Journal of Business,* Vol. 46 (October 1973): 554–73.

Jain, P. C. "The Effect of Voluntary Sell-off Announcements on Shareholders' Wealth." *Journal of Finance,* Vol. 40 (March 1985): 209–24.

Jensen, M. "The Performance of Mutual Funds in the Period 1945-1964." *Journal of Finance,* Vol. 23 (May 1968): 389–416.

Jensen, M., and Meckling, W. "Theory of the Firm: Managerial Behavior, Agency Costs and Ownership Structure." *Journal of Financial Economics,* Vol. 3 (March 1976): 305–60.

Klein, A. "The Timing and Substance of Divestiture Announcements: Individual, Simultaneous and Cumulative Effects." *Journal of Finance,* Vol. 41 (July 1986): 685–96.

Kolodny, R., Laurence, M., and Ghosh, Arabinda "In Search of Excellence . . . for Whom?" *Journal of Portfolio Management,* Vol. 15 (Spring 1989): 56–60.

Lewellen, W. "Management and Ownership in the Large Firm." *Journal of Finance,* Vol. 24 (May 1969) 299–322.

Markowitz, H. "Portfolion Selection." *Journal of Finance,* Vol. 7 (March 1952): 77–91.

Miles, J. A., and Rosenfeld, J. D. "The Effect of Voluntary Spin-off Announcements on Shareholder Wealth." *Journal of Finance,* Vol. 37 (December 1983): 1597–1606.

Miller, M. "Debt and Taxes." *Journal of Finance,* Vol. 32 (May 1977): 261–75.

Modigliani, F., and Miller, M. "The Cost of Capital, Corporation Finance and the Theory of Investments." *American Economic Review,* Vol. 48 (June 1958): 261–97.

Murphy, K. "Corporate Performance and Managerial Remuneration: An Empirical Analysis." *Journal of Accounting & Economics,* Vol. 7 (April 1985): 11–42.

Sharpe, W. "Capital-Asset Prices: A Theory of Market Equilibrium under Condition of Risk." *Journal of Finance,* Vol. 19 (Sept. 1964): 425–42.

Sharpe, W. "Mutual Fund Performance." *Journal of Business,* Vol. 39 (January 1966): 119–38.

Treynor, J. "How to Rate Management of Investment Funds." *Harvard Business Review,* Vol. 43 (Jan.-Feb. 1965): 63–75.

# Index

# About the Author

ARABINDA GHOSH is an Associate Professor of Economics and Finance at the School of Management, William Paterson College in New Jersey. He is the author of *OPEC, the Petroleum Industry and United States Energy Policy* (1983), and *Competition and Diversification in the United States Petroleum Industry* (1985). His articles have appeared in such publications as *The Wall Street Journal, The Oil Daily, The Antitrust Bulletin, The Indian Economic Journal, The Journal of Industrial Economics, The Journal of Portfolio Management,* and *The North American Review of Economics and Finance.*